MW00528168

THERE'S SOMETHING
I WANT TO TELL YOU

THERE'S SOMETHING
I WANT TO TELL YOU
TRUE STORIES OF MIXED
DATING
IN JAPAN
YUTA AOKI

There's Something I Want to Tell You: True Stories of Mixed Dating in Japan
Copyright © 2015 by Yuta Aoki. All rights reserved.
First Print Edition: January 2015
ISBN: 978-4-9908188-0-7

Formatting: Blue Valley Author Services

No part of this book may be reproduced, scanned, or distributed in any printed or electronic form without permission. Please do not participate in or encourage piracy of copyrighted materials in violation of the author's rights. Thank you for respecting the hard work of this author.

This book is based on interviews and the author does not necessarily support all the opinions and statements expressed by the interviewees. Some names and identifying details have been changed to protect the privacy of individuals.

Table of Contents

Free Extra Chapter

As a thank you gift to my readers, I am offering a free extra
chapter:

**Takuya and Annie—If you really like her, you won't
give up easily**
(How a Japanese guy won a Swedish girl's heart)

You can download this chapter for free at:
http://www.yutaaoki.com/ts-extra

Introduction

Why Jasmine is unhappy

"SORRY, I'M ITALIAN. WE'RE LATE for everything," Jasmine texted me. Apparently, she was lost in the middle of Shinjuku, one of Tokyo's busiest districts. Earlier, I had made sure she knew where the Japanese discount store Don Quixote was. I had even sent her a map.

She texted me again. "I'm near Forever 21. Which way do I go?"

"All right, stay where you are. I'm coming," I answered.

As soon as she saw me, she said, "I learned a lesson: never think I'm smart. Next time I meet someone, I need to say to myself, 'Jasmine, you are not smart.'"

She was an Italian-American from New York, petite and fit. I could easily imagine a lot of Asian guys being into her.

But Jasmine was unhappy.

In the States, she'd been popular. "From eighteen to twenty-three, I think the longest I was single was about four months. It was really, really easy," she said.

She had dated a Japanese-American guy in the States.

"Both his parents were from Japan. His first language was Japanese because his father didn't speak English well, and neither did his mother. I met him online. We were together for about a year and a half.

"He was a digital artist. He actually had a little bit of a job working on *Final Fantasy XI*, I think. I was into video games, and he liked manga. He had those pop culture things that Japanese people get to enjoy. We went to a Dir en Grey (a Japanese metal band) show together because they were our favorite band. We went to Hikaru Utada's concert as well. We had a lot in common.

"It was a really good relationship. But I broke up with him, because I realized I wasn't in love with him. I started to really look inward and discovered that in my heart, I didn't love him. But I knew he loved me."

"Have you always liked Asian guys?"

"I have only dated Asian guys. I'm just really, really attracted to them! I have nothing against other guys, but if somebody says, 'What's your favorite ice cream?' I will scream 'Mint chocolate chip!' So when somebody offers you mint chocolate chip or chocolate chip, which one would you take? You take mint chocolate chip of course! There were plenty of guys who had Asian backgrounds on my campus. So I just always went after what I wanted and I always got what I wanted."

But she hasn't found a boyfriend in Japan.

"I've been single since I came here two years ago. It's really depressing. I don't have trouble getting asked out online. I have been on a lot of low-key coffee dates. I found the guys physically attractive, but nothing about their personalities jumped out at me. I'm someone with a huge personality. So I don't want to be with somebody mediocre.

"I've been on OKCupid for a year. Two weeks ago, my friend asked me casually, 'Do you have an OKCupid profile?' I said, 'Yeah, I've had one for a while. Why?' My friend said, 'One guy asked me if you were on it, because he said you looked familiar.' Lately, I am getting approached by a lot of guys saying they've seen me on OKCupid. I'm like, 'Oh man, I'm becoming an OKCupid celebrity!' That's not something to brag about at all.

"In person, I only get approached when I miss my train and I am waiting for a taxi outside Ikebukuro Station. But the guys who approach me are all drunk businessmen. I always think, 'Excuse me, I'm waiting for my taxi. It's a quarter to one at night. I'm tired. You're old. See you later.'

"I've always considered myself an attractive person. But, not being asked out in a long time, it kind of makes me feel a little insecure. One thing that prevents me from building a rapport with Japanese guys is my personality, because I don't act Japanese. I'm very outgoing and very energetic."

"Can't that be seen as a part of your charm?"

"I haven't got that impression. I feel like many Japanese guys are put off by my personality. So I think, 'Oh, I'm too loud and maybe I'm too aggressive.'"

So, is dating in Japan that hard?

In this book, you will learn how people come to Japan and have successful—or unsuccessful—dating lives.

You will read about a British guy who saved a Japanese girl from a robber, an American girl who approached a cute guy in a student building, a Russian girl who met her husband in a Roppongi club, and many more.

If you are new to Japan, this is the perfect book for you! The stories in this book are full of cultural insights and lessons, and reading them will give you a head start on Japanese dating culture.

The people in this book are diverse. Its contributors come from the US, the UK, Finland, Russia, Kenya, the Philippines, Jamaica, and Japan, and include straight, gay, and bisexual people.

Welcome to dating in Japan!

1. Nadia—Almost getting picked up on the street

How a black girl from North Carolina met her fiancé

NADIA WAS WALKING ON THE street in her neighborhood in Gunma (a prefecture north of Tokyo). She was going to a birthday party. It was a small town, and she knew the place well.

A car came up behind her and pulled over.

"Hey, what's up?" a guy shouted at her. He said it in clear English. He was a Japanese guy. He smiled.

"Uh, *konbanwa*?" Nadia said.

The whole situation made her uncomfortable. The sun was already going down. There was no way she would stop to talk to him.

She walked away, thinking she would never meet him again.

That was how she met her fiancé.

———◄ ♥ ►———

"I hear a lot of women say that Japanese men are shy, but I tend not to meet those men," Nadia said. "I used to come to Shibuya by myself and someone would always stop and talk to me. Guys do that all the time. My friends don't believe me when I tell them. But when they are with me and see guys approaching me, I say, 'I told you so!'

"Sometimes, a car passes me two or three times, then it pulls up, and the driver asks me to get in. That makes me nervous. It happened in Asakusa, Ebisu, and Akasaka. In Akasaka, I was walking back to the hotel pretty late at night. The driver was a much, much older man. The younger guys actually come up to me and talk. Most of the time they speak English because they have lived abroad.

"I went up to Saitama once, to Kumagaya—about an hour from Tokyo. I got the best *nampa* (an attempt to pick up a girl) ever. He was so good at it that I went home and told my fiancé. I was walking from Kumagaya station, and this guy kind of popped out of nowhere.

"He said, 'Sorry, can I ask you a question? Do you speak Japanese? I don't live around here but I really want to go to a good pasta restaurant. Do you know a good place?'

"I said, 'I just moved here. But if you go down this street, you'll have a lot of choices.'

'Oh great, that sounds good. Hey, are you really busy?'

'No.'

'I was just looking at you and you are very cool. Your hair. Your style. You are so beautiful. If you have time I'd love to take you out to eat.'

'Thank you, but I have a boyfriend.'

'I understand. How long have you been together?'

'Six years.'

'Oh. If you had said a year, I would have kept trying. Six years, you probably love this guy.'

"There were a lot of people around, but the way he did it was so impressive. I told my fiancé about this and he asked, 'If you were single, would you have gone out with him?' I said, 'Hell yeah!' He was good looking too, probably about thirty-five."

The banker guy

"I was at a coffee shop with a guy I met online. The conversation was very light: question, answer, question, answer. It had been two weeks since I first met him. I sat down a little closer next to him on the coffee shop couch. He got up and went to the other side of the table—he was uncomfortable being so close.

"He was ten or twelve years older than me. He lived in Saitama and he was a bank manager in Tokyo. He looked very stiff. He translated contracts from English to Japanese, so he understood written English, but he couldn't speak it very well. Our conversation started out something like, 'I need someone to teach me English.'

"I asked him why he picked me. He was fairly wealthy and he could have hired a personal coach. He said, 'I want to learn English, and you are cute. It's like killing two birds with one stone.' He was actually quite funny. He would ask me English questions, and a question might be about some erotic lyrics and we would laugh about it. He would relax and start to smile.

"He asked me how it felt teaching Japanese children and I told him about the *kancho* (a kind of prank Japanese children play on each other. You hold your middle fingers together and poke somebody's anus). I'd never experienced anything like that in my life. He was like, 'Yeah it's pretty gross, but as a kid it's really fun to do.' And he added, 'If I quit my job, I'm going to do that to my boss.' We laughed

7

so hard that he was almost crying. He had this dream of quitting his job and opening up a ramen shop.

"For the way he looked, he had amazing musical taste, like hard-core punk. He liked anything from hip-hop to death metal. He liked Argentinean punk groups. At work, he didn't let anything out about his personal life. When we were together, we would always go to another city, because he didn't want to run into people he knew and neither did I."

"Did he make a move?"

"One time, we were walking and laughing, and he put his arm around my shoulders. But then he put his hand down as if he were suddenly thinking, *oh wait, I forgot what I was doing*. For three seconds, he was a human. I asked him what was sexy to him. He said, 'Going to a night club and seeing a woman just dancing by herself with a drink in her hand, not giving a fuck.' He actually wrote that. A lot of time he would get nervous and start to write. I thought that was interesting because I couldn't see him going to a club. But he liked traveling and when he got sent off to Singapore for work, he would go out to the market all by himself as soon as the meeting was over.

"We communicated for a while, but it was just too hard. He was saving his money because he wanted to quit his job. He still lived with his dad and his brother. I knew he made a lot of money, but instead of living the high life, he was living in the countryside. I actually liked him. I would have loved to kiss him."

The Citadel guy

Before she met her fiancé, she'd dated another guy.

"We met online. There was something so interesting about him. I asked him, 'How did you learn English?' and he said he went to the Citadel, the top military academy in

THERE'S SOMETHING I WANT TO TELL YOU

the US. It's a soldier school! What the hell? I had to know how this happened. I thought you had to be a US citizen to go there.

"He spoke perfect English. He was also very artsy and kind of hippy. He did an African dance and played the drums. I met his sister, who was also interesting. She was always going to Cuba. She was a salsa dancer. She didn't speak English or even Spanish, but the girl could dance her ass off. She wanted to get married. She was like forty at the time and never married but she was fucking her dad's friend. They were both unconventional.

"It was an interesting family. They had a family business, and my boyfriend was the youngest brother. His older brother was the president, but he was the one who knew English, so he handled all of the international business.

"We ended it pretty badly because he was unreliable. Having a family business meant he was busy, so we had to plan our dates a few weeks in advance. But he would either show up or call right before we were supposed to meet and say, 'I can't come.' A few times, something happened at work and he would go out with one of his boys. Then he would drunk-dial me. He was so rude to me. He'd say, 'I don't care. Don't expect me to treat you well.' And I'd say, 'You know what? I hope you die. You are a horrible person.'

"But afterwards, he was so sorry about the way he had treated me. He had run into his friend later and his friend said, 'What the hell? She is a great girl,' so he tried to get me back.

"I didn't realize this at the time, but there was a red flag. He said, 'I don't have any foreign friends,' even though he graduated from a US university. He said, 'Foreigners are weird.' I don't think that at any point he had really tried to learn about another culture. Everything we did, we disagreed about something. He would immediately became passive-aggressive and said something like, 'That's what Japanese people do.' I knew that wasn't true, because I was working with Japanese people. Japanese people were supposed to be on time, but he wasn't."

Kazuki

Then she met her fiancé, Kazuki, in an unexpected way.

"He saw me walking when he was driving a car. He slowed down and said, 'Hey what's up?' I heard it in really clear English. I looked at him and he was smiling. I think I said, 'Konbanwa.' But I wasn't going to stop, because he was with all these dudes around. I didn't feel comfortable.

"Later on, I was at a birthday party. It was at a bar and the building had two floors. I was on the second floor. I got a call and my friend said, 'You should come downstairs. I want to introduce you to somebody.' So I went downstairs.

"My friend was there and there was a Japanese guy sitting next to her. I thought, *he's the guy from the car*! She introduced us and Kazuki introduced himself in English. I was older by three years. He said he was really drunk when he approached me. I had thought he was perfectly sober. He seemed nice and said, 'Can I email you sometime?'

"The party was like a DJ party in a store. He had a friend who was a DJ and the DJ was having a party for promotion. It was a hip-hop clothing store and every time I walked by, a guy with an Afro perm said hello. It was a small town, so I walked the same street every day when I went to work.

"Kazuki lived in Saitama, but he was just randomly meeting his friends in Gunma. He didn't go there a lot. He's definitely a Saitama boy, not cosmopolitan like Tokyo guys. He said I reminded him of Foxy Brown. I was flattered. He'd been in Canada for a little over a year trying to learn English and had just got back to Japan.

"The next day, he emailed me with all these smiley faces. He wrote, 'I love talking to you. I'd like to take you out on a date.'

"We went on our first date the following weekend. We talked about music. He liked really good stuff like jazz or Pink Floyd. I was concerned because I'd met a lot of guys who were into hip-hop and just wanted to go out with black girls. But he had a really well-rounded musical taste.

"Kazuki came to my belly dance show. At the time, occasionally, I would hang out with my ex-boyfriend who was trying to get back together with me, even though I wasn't interested. I had invited my ex-boyfriend to the show way before, so my first date was with Kazuki and my ex-boyfriend together. It was weird. The place was a Peruvian-owned bar and after everybody had left, they played merengue, so I danced with the owner. And those two were sitting together watching me dance with another guy.

"I decided to stay out the whole night in Tokyo. So the three of us went to eat. Everything was fine and we were all speaking English because my Japanese at the time was pretty sad.

"Then I had to go to the bathroom. When I came back, they were speaking Japanese and that's when it got awkward. Kazuki was trying to figure out the situation. He was like, 'OK, this guy isn't some random dude. What the hell?' They were continuing in Japanese and I couldn't catch any of it.

"I took the train back with Kazuki and he got off in Saitama. Then the next week we went out, just the two of us.

"He came to pick me up and we went to a little local restaurant. The restaurant had a relaxed atmosphere. They had couches. We actually sat down next to each other. I didn't go there that much, because I hated the owner. But he thought those spaces were cool and the only other option was the place where we met, but everybody knew us there.

11

"We just talked. I thought it was interesting that I had a beer, but he didn't because he was driving. But then he emailed the guy who introduced us, asking, 'Can I stay at your place tonight?' The guy said yes, so he drank.

"We must have stayed out pretty late. It was about three in the morning. I went to give him a hug. While I was hugging him, he kissed me. We got really embarrassed after. I wasn't expecting it. When we passed that hip-hop shop, they said to him, 'Oh, you are going out with her!'

"He wanted us to be boyfriend and girlfriend. But I said no for a few months. On our third date, when we were just eating out, he said, 'I'm going to marry you.' It wasn't creepy, but he said it very randomly. The conversation wasn't even about the relationship! It was as if he'd said, 'Hey, the sky is blue today. By the way, I'm going to marry you.' So I was like, 'Oh, look! I see a cloud,' and just carried on the conversation. We never spoke about that afterwards."

"What's your fiancé like? What are his interests?"

"He likes boxing, jiu jitsu, photography, and fashion. He is a mechanical forklift operator. He got his license in Canada. But his job has been changing and he'll be a manager. He does a lot of paperwork now and he doesn't like it. Lately, he gets off around ten."

"Did he go to university?"

"No. He was working for a supermarket delivering groceries when I met him. A lot of his friends—they are all pretty much Japanese—don't speak English and haven't been abroad. But at the same time, they are definitely different. When I met them, it wasn't as if they were thinking, 'Oh, the foreign girl!' I was just his girlfriend. I never felt 'othered' by them. A lot of them had tattoos (which are not common in Japan), so maybe in some ways they have outside-the-box thinking. Usually, if I go someplace in the countryside, people say things like, 'Can you use chopsticks? Wow, you are so different!' But not his friends.

"One thing they have common is music and dancing. They are very artistic. A lot of them play musical instruments quite well. One guy is a math teacher but he is a hell of a b-boy (a hip-hop breakdancer). They are in bands on weekends, but they go to work in suits. Some of them are DJs and a lot of them play the djembe. Kazuki even plays the didgeridoo!"

It took them a while to become boyfriend and girlfriend.

"We were at a friend's birthday party and we were having a picnic. That was the first time I brought him to meet my friends. There were a lot of foreigners there and he was very nervous. He was very quiet and sat very close to me the whole time.

"After the picnic, he said, 'I always have fun with you. You are so cool.'

"I said, 'You are cool too.'

'But not enough to be my girlfriend.'

'Are you asking?'

"He had kind of hinted before, but I was thinking I wasn't ready.

"He said, 'If I ask, what will you say?'

'Why don't you ask?'

'I would like you to be my girlfriend.'

'OK.'

'Really?'

"Then he got half-naked and did flips. He was openly happy.

"Soon after, I let him spend the night with me. In the beginning, we pretty much spent at least one day together on a weekend, the whole day. When he wanted to see me during the week, he would have to spend the night and leave my house at five am to get to work. We've continued that for the past seven years. We still do that.

"Culture-wise, one time, I was pretending to be difficult. We were eating and he wanted something. I was like, 'No, you can't have it. I'm tired.' Then he said, 'Bitch!' I know he didn't mean it. Maybe he had picked that up from some movie. I said, 'Don't say that.' But he said it again. I got pretty upset. I said, 'This can be a deal breaker for us. It's that serious. Don't ever say that to me again.' Then he was like, 'Oh, OK, now I get it.'

"When he's in a really bad mood, he mumbles. It's not a language issue. He thinks the problem is his English. But the real problem is not opening his mouth. I think that's his personal insecurity.

"Early on, we used to have disagreements about everything. He'd claim something like, 'Oh, I can't get along with you, because your culture is different.' Every time something happened that would happen in any normal relationship, he thought it was something cultural. He'd say, 'Because they have a big penis and I don't.' I find men are pretty much the same across every culture.

"What I like about him is that when he says he's going to do something, he's going to do it. He had some friends invite him out, but he was sick and tired from work, so he didn't want to go. I said, 'You can just tell your friends that you are going to stay in for tonight.' But he said, 'I can't do that, because they want me to come.'

"I obviously like Japanese culture, but I think certain things are not good. When I'd say that I don't like something about Japan, initially he took it really personally. He would be a bit defensive. We were talking about junior idols (in Japan, teenage idol girl groups tend to be popular). Some of them look about thirteen years old and that was really disgusting to me. Then he'd say, 'If you don't like it, why do you live here?' I was like, 'OK, calm down. I'm not saying all Japan is like that.'

"He didn't understand that I had been discriminated against. His attitude was, 'I'm not sure if that happens in Japan.'

"I said, 'Yeah, it does.'

'If Japanese people discriminate against you, why do you live here?'

'Well, Americans discriminate against me.'

"He saw it for the first time and he was like, 'Oh, wow.' Now he is with me.

"I remember he was talking about a 'scary black guy' and I was like 'Hello? Black? Think about what you say about my father, my uncle.' And then he realized it. He gets it now."

Getting engaged wasn't a smooth process for Nadia.

"I knew he was getting serious, because he started to get a little bit more worried about how our relationship would be viewed. He's never worried about his friends, but he was worried about his colleagues."

"I do remember that gradually, over time, we realized that we talked about our future unconsciously. We were both using 'we.'

"After about three or four years, my contract with the JET program (a government-sponsored program in which English speakers are sent to teach English in Japanese schools) ended. I needed to find a new job. There was a job in Chiba, but I was still looking locally because we wanted to stay together. So we sat down and talked about it. Chiba didn't seem too far for me, because I was from a bigger country, but the distance felt greater for him. I said, 'If you want me to stay. I'll take this crazy low-paying job here.' But he said, 'No, take the better job in Chiba and we can save up for our future.' So I decided to go to Chiba.

"It turned out he had some resentment that I moved. He said, 'I couldn't be direct about it. I couldn't tell you not to move.' I said, 'I asked you if it would be a problem. I could have taken a lower paying job there, because you are more important to me than my job.' But we had a big argument about that. Up until then, we had never had an argument.

"He said, 'Let's move in together.' But I told him, 'Let me think about it. Because if we're not getting married, I don't see the point.'

"Then there were his parents. He didn't tell me that his parents were not cool about me. When I asked him, 'Do your parents know about this?' he made it seem as though they were not against it. But he had never invited me to his house. He'd say, 'I don't take girls to my house.' But I said, 'You took your female friend to your house!' Then it came out that it was because I was a foreigner. I told him, 'You are going to have to tell them, because if they don't accept me, I'll need to make my decision whether I'm going to be with you or not.'

"He started to get really nervous about making a formal announcement to his parents. He started getting cold feet. I was thinking, *Seriously, there's a limit. If you can't say anything, I'm not going to hang around hoping that you get the balls to say something.* I didn't say this, but I thought we might just actually break up. I started preparing myself for that.

"One day, we had a huge fight, and I left the house and went for a walk. It was raining. I must have stayed out for a good five hours. I didn't take my phone with me. He was pissed off but worried. I came back, and he was still awake. I went to my bedroom and shut the door. I fell asleep.

"He came in and sat next to me and tried to hug me. It was around three am. I said, 'Don't touch me.' He said, 'I want to be with you.' I didn't like being strung along, because too many people in Japan are in a relationship for a long time and then, after five or six years, the other person drops the bomb and says 'I can't marry a non-Japanese person.' He told me, 'It's not like that. I know I definitely want to be with you. I'm just worried about my family.' I said, 'That's fine, but you deal with it.' I was thinking that if we didn't get married within a year, it would be over. But I didn't tell him this. To this day, he still doesn't know.

"What I didn't know was that he had actually been doing something. I had met his cousins and aunt, but I didn't know they were family. He had been kind of introducing me to everybody around his parents and then trying to get back to them. But he never expressed it to me. I had no idea that some of the people I had been meeting were so close to him. Knowing that would have actually helped.

"Pretty soon after that, I met his family. I ended up having dinner with his mom. His mom turned out to be nervous and she brought her best friend along! After about ten minutes, we were relaxed. Then she suddenly said, 'I want my children to have wedding ceremonies in Hawaii.'

"She asked me, 'What kind of visa do you have?' I thought it was a strange question. But it occurred to me that she was worried I was just trying to marry him to stay in Japan. She wanted to make sure that it was legitimate. Well, it's the same thing for my mom because when I had foreign boyfriends in the States, my mom asked me, 'Does he want to live in the States?'

"Once that was over, I got invited to their house. I asked his mom about typical Japanese cooking and we clicked over that. Actually, we are kind of similar. We both like to travel and we both like the actor Yutaka Takenouchi. She had a big poster of him on the wall. Kazuki had told her I loved him, and she got really excited.

"She picked up that I liked red. She got me really cool earrings. We kind of have the same taste. I think it really helped that I could speak Japanese. She had been to Hawaii but never the mainland US. She had been to Paris, Rome, and Madrid and had romantic images of Europe, but her images of the US weren't very good. But eventually she grew relaxed. 'Oh, Nadia is normal.'"

"How did you meet his dad?"

"I was invited to their house. The first time, his dad wasn't there. And then the second time, his dad invited us for *suppon* (soft-shelled turtle) cuisine for dinner. That was good. At first, he was quiet. Then Kazuki said I had a Honda. His dad worked for Honda, and I think he was in Sales. I said, 'That's the best car ever.' Then he started relaxing and talking. He was perfectly friendly, but he still looked nervous. He noticed I was using my left hand and said, 'Oh, southpaw.' He spoke a little English with me!"

"Was there any particular moment that he actually proposed?"

"He actually did the on-the-knees thing a few weeks ago. He said, 'I want to get you a ring, because in America, you are supposed to get a ring.' But I didn't really give a shit. I said, 'Let's save the money for a house. Who cares?' He said, 'No, I want to get you a ring.'

"His mom also told him to get me a ring. His mom found a wholesale jeweler and set up an appointment for us. He said, 'I want to take you with me. I'm scared. I won't like it if there's something wrong.' He had this thing about numbers, so he said, 'I'm going to get you three stones.' We went to the jeweler and designed a ring with ruby in the middle and three diamonds on each side. It was still spring.

"At the time he was asking, 'How do you do the wedding proposal in America?' I thought he was just curious. We looked at people doing big wedding proposals on YouTube. You know, stuff like dancing or flash mobs. I said, 'That's just crazy.' And we laughed. His Japanese friend had just done a b-boy flash mob proposal. Another friend did it at his

18

concert. That was pretty much American style. But I think I didn't mention the fact that not everybody does that in America.

"A long time had passed. One day, I asked, 'You need to check out those rings, because they are supposed to be ready. Have you even called them?'

"He started to say, 'Well... I think... maybe...'

'What's wrong?'

'They're in my car!'

'In the car? Did you forget the ring in the car or something? It's been weeks!'

'I'm just really stressed out about this proposal thing! I've been trying to find a nice place and set something up.'

'What? Have I ever been that showy kind of person?'

'But that's what Americans do!'

'No! I was just showing you what other people do.'

'Yeah, but I thought I had to do that.'

"He actually had planned to do it at one of the events we went to, but he got cold feet.

"He said, 'OK, can I do it now?' I said, 'Sure.' I was in pajamas. He ran out to the car, brought the ring and said, 'Will you marry me?' I was like, 'Obviously?' We drank some beer and updated our Facebook.

"I didn't want a wedding. Let's put that on the record. This is for the mothers. My mom pretends I've never said that. My dad heard it. Kazuki heard it. Even his mom heard it, but his mom also wanted us to get married in Hawaii. And my mom said, 'Wedding in Hawaii? That's a great idea!'

"I had a friend who had gotten married in Hawaii. Her husband is Japanese. I got info from her and looked online. In my mind, we were paying for the wedding, but then my dad said, 'I'll pay for it.' I wouldn't say that was a problem, but I knew that in Japan the cost is kind of shared. So his

19

parents were thinking, *we should do something*. They were a little bit worried about it.

"Actually, I want to talk to his mom today, because I don't want her to think that I'm not including her. I don't really know how you are supposed to do it, but Kazuki can't really help me. It seems that even in Japan, the bride and their mom kind of do everything for the most part. But he's asking me questions and I'm saying, 'I have never been married. How would I know this?'"

Discussions

There might be some cultural reasons why Nadia's fiancé was reluctant to talk to his parents about their relationship. Japanese people—especially men—don't always discuss relationships with their parents, and it is not uncommon to meet your boyfriend or girlfriend's parents for the first time after you get engaged.

There's another possible cultural issue: initially, Nadia's fiancé's parents weren't quite up for the marriage. Japan is a highly homogeneous country where 98.5% of the people are considered to be of the same ethnicity, and most Japanese people don't usually have much exposure to people from outside Japan. Some parents may feel uncertain about their children marrying internationally, simply because of their fear of the unknown.

There is one other interesting episode concerning Nadia and her fiancé. Once, I hung out with Nadia at a Jamaican festival in Yoyogi Park and we very randomly ran into her fiancé. Apparently, neither was expecting to see the other. Interestingly, her fiancé was with a girl from Botswana. So there we were, him hanging out with a girl and her with a guy (me). They were pretty cool about the situation. We chatted a little bit and said goodbye.

2. Charles—He didn't speak Japanese; she didn't speak English

How a British guy managed to marry a non-westernized Japanese girl

W HEN I MET CHARLES FOR the first time, he was wearing a cute T-shirt with a large sunny side up egg printed on it. 'Hey, nice T-shirt,' I said, but I wasn't really paying too much attention to him, because I was trying to talk to some girl.

But Charles started asking me questions.

"What kind of 80s music are you into?" he asked.

"Well, I don't know. I grew up with 90s music."

"Oh, what artists did you listen to then?"

I didn't understand why he was so eager to discuss music with me. I would rather have been talking to the girl.

Charles turned out to be a perfectly nice guy. He was soft spoken and friendly. He was working in the music industry, and that's why he was so eager to discuss music.

But most importantly, he had a very interesting dating story.

Early girlfriends

"I was incredibly, painfully shy. When I was in my early teens, I couldn't look people in the eye. I was the sort of kid who would walk along the street reading a book. I loved reading magazines and playing video games.

"Actually, I had quite a lot of girlfriends when I was a kid. Even when I was very little, there would be girls down the street. When I was about sixteen, I had this girlfriend. She had a really lovely family. We were together for a couple of years.

"She once had a go at me. We were at her family friend's house. I was being a little bit antisocial and shy. She said, 'You've got to stop being shy because it's rude.' That was sort of a turning point. After that, I made a conscious effort to come out of my shell. Now I have no problem at all. By the time I was in my late teens I was more easy-going.

"My first proper girlfriend was probably when I was fourteen. I really liked her. I used to just go around to her house and if we wanted privacy, we would either go around to one of our houses when no one was home or to a local park. We hung out quite a lot in parks because there were a lot of parks in London. They usually shut the park in the evening, but there was always a way to get in at night. It's also quite easy to get alcohol when you are underage in England."

"How were you able to attract girls even though you were shy?"

"I don't know. Shared taste in music had something to do with it. Or having the same group of friends."

But I can guess why. He has handsome, pale, sensitive features. He also has such a beautiful voice with a North

London accent (not to be confused with the Cockney variant). And he sounds very caring when he speaks.

The fanzine girl

"I had a girlfriend when I was about eighteen for a couple of years. She came to see one of the bands I was playing in. We had a gig at a tiny venue. She had a fanzine. She just came up and said, 'I want to write about your band.' So she interviewed me. That was the start of it.

"She was into the same music as I was. We would go to small, local gigs. We drank loads and loads of tea. I was quite lucky, because both her parents and my parents were fairly easy-going."

"Did she have the same kind of background?"

"She was similar. Her dad had died and her mother had brought her up alone. Her mom was Polish and her dad was Pakistani. Very strange mix. Her mom hadn't remarried but had a boyfriend who was a very stereotypically Jewish Londoner. My girlfriend was very much into music and also a bit of an outsider. She went off to university and broke up with me."

Coming to Japan

"Were you already interested in Japan before you came here?"

"A little bit. I was into Shonen Knife (a Japanese girl band). When I was in university, I had a Japanese friend and I told her about Shonen Knife and she said, 'If you like Shonen Knife, here's a Puffy CD.' I started getting into other things. She had a very large CD collection and she was crazy about music. She let me look at her copies of *Rockin'on* magazine that her mom sent her every month. She got me into Tamio Okuda and Tama as well. We went out for a few months.

"After her, I happened to be with another Japanese girl who lived in London. She lived in a house with loads of other Japanese and Chinese people, and I used to spend all my time hanging out with them. Some of them are still my best friends. We would just sit around all day long playing Xbox. At that time I was working, but most of them were still students.

"My girlfriend had just graduated. She wanted to figure out what she wanted to do in her life. Originally, she was studying somewhere else in England, but once she had finished, she moved to London. I think she was just living off her parents' support for a little while after she finished university. She might have had a part-time job too. We went out for a few months.

"At the time, I hadn't been to Japan. Everywhere I'd been was in Europe or America. I think the way I imagined Japanese culture was completely naive and off base. Everything I knew about Japan was what I learned from these people. I noticed they were a little bit shy compared to Londoners. They were always very honest and polite. Whenever we had house parties and finished late at night, it was always Japanese people who got mugged on the way home! They were kind of easy targets.

"Japanese people who live overseas or even who have been overseas are in the minority. Statistically, many people in Japan don't have a passport. When we help Japanese bands go overseas, part of the process is getting them passports first.

"It takes a certain mentality to live overseas. The Japanese friends I had in England were very interested in cultural stuff. They chose England usually because they were into British music or sometimes their schools were tied up with

British universities. Or sometimes they didn't like American culture.

"Here's something I noticed that was quite common among my Japanese friends: they said the reason they came to London or enjoyed England was because it was free. I never really understood that until I came to Japan and lived here for a few years. There is an incredible amount of peer pressure, which I am sure I don't feel anywhere near as much as somebody who was born here. There is a constant feeling of being judged based on your actions. You take out the rubbish on the wrong day, you are an asshole."

"Why did Japan attract you?"

"The music was a big thing. It was getting to the point where a lot of my favorite music was Judy and Mary, Seagull Screaming Kiss Her Kiss Her, Cornelius, Guitar Wolf, or Poly 6. None of my British friends had a clue about these bands. None of the people in the industry knew what I was talking about. People who did understand were my Japanese friends. Not only could they talk about it, they could also show me more bands.

"When I was twenty-five or twenty-six, I worked for a very famous company in Britain. People there were really nice and talented. I'd been freelancing for a long time and that was the first full-time job I even wanted to go for. But after four months they cancelled the project I was involved in.

"I was going out with a girl at the time. We were living together, and were thinking about buying a house together. We'd been together for two years. But we broke up. Three days later, my project was cancelled. A friend of mine had been saying, 'I'd like to go to Japan for six months. We should go together.' But I'd been saying, 'I can't. I really love my job.' It was just fate. I had to do it now. I was just inside the age limit bracket. So, I applied for a working holiday visa. I went to the Japanese embassy with all the documents, waited for about ten minutes and they said, 'That's fine. Come back in two weeks and you'll have your visa.' It was so easy, it was unbelievable. It only cost around twenty pounds.

"I moved here and I had a friend who helped me find an apartment. I was hanging out with my friends every day, and very, very quickly, I made friends with a lot of people. I was excited to be able to see all those bands I liked. Most bands that were popular in Britain were not popular in Japan.

"Those days, you stood out as a foreigner, especially when you were into alternative music. In 2006, when you went to live houses (small live music venues), you didn't see any foreigners. Certain people would just come up and start a conversation because they thought you were interesting. I dated a few people here, but none of the relationships were that major.

"There was a bar near my house. It was right next to a recording studio so it was always full of musicians. It was the kind of bar where there were only seven or eight seats, and a DJ booth taking up half the space. I used to go there every night, because I wanted to learn Japanese. All my friends in Japan already spoke English. But in that bar, nobody did.

"I was freelancing for companies in the UK for a little while. When I had been here for six months, I got a job and started working for a Japanese company. It was pretty easy. It was difficult for them to find someone who was living in Japan, staying long term, and who had professional experience. The pool wasn't actually big. I was already one of the most experienced people."

The drummer's friend

"I made friends with one of the members of a Japanese band. One day, I was at a restaurant in Yoyogi having a meeting with a band manager about taking the band to the UK. The drummer walked into the pub. I thought she was quite nice. I kind of wanted to stick around and hang out with her, but once the meeting was finished, they walked me to the station. It was sort of a Japanese hospitality thing, but I was an adult!

"A few days later, I got a text from the singer in the band, saying, 'We're going out next weekend. The drummer is bringing one of her friends along. Do you want to come?' The singer knew I was trying to find a proper girlfriend.

"We went to a bar run by a famous musician. It was like a secret bar. The woman who owned the bar also knew that I had this thing going on. She arranged the seating in such a way that we would end up sitting next to each other.

"The drummer turned up with her friend. My first impression of that girl was that she was very fashionably dressed even though she was a musician. Usually, musicians just turned up in a T-shirt. She came in and sat down. She had a nice smile.

"But at that time, my Japanese wasn't very good. I had just taken my first lesson that day. I'd been in Japan for a year, so I picked up a fair amount by studying at home and through going out drinking. It was enough to get by, but I couldn't really have any meaningful conversation. And she didn't speak any English at all. She'd never had any foreign friends except for one who spoke fluent Japanese.

"Despite that, we somehow managed to have a conversation, obviously aided by my friends and also alcohol. As we were chatting, we discovered a lot of weird coincidences, like our birthdays were one day apart. We just got on very well. She gave me her CD, which I thought was really cool. She was a singer-songwriter and guitarist. We ended up chatting until three or four in the morning."

"Do you think she was already interested in you?"

"No! The next day, I listened to her CD and liked it a lot. She had a very unusual singing voice and I really liked that. I listened to it endlessly for a week. Then I emailed her saying, 'Hey, let's go out again sometime,' and she emailed me back saying, 'No, thanks.'

"And then a friend got me a couple of tickets to go and see UA (a Japanese female artist) so I asked, 'Hey do you want to see UA?' I knew she liked UA. She said, 'All right.'

"It was an outdoor gig in Hibiya Park. It was really, really long. We were sitting on stone seats and UA played for two hours. In the middle of it, she had a thing about climate change for thirty minutes. I was thinking, *oh my god. My arse hurts so much in this seat. I just want to talk to this girl I'm with instead.*

"It was a daytime show and we ended up spontaneously spending the whole day together. There was a restaurant in the park and we had ice cream there. We wandered around the park and went to karaoke. She was a rock musician but she loved *enka* (old Japanese style pop music, usually popular among elderly people). She sang Sayuri Ishikawa's (famous *enka* singer) song. She's got such an amazing voice. You know that kind of vibrato that *enka* singers use? She could do that. And then we went to an *izakaya* and drank sake. She was saying how much she liked sake, and I liked sake too.

"But it took a couple of months before anything really happened. We would meet up every now and then, and we always had a good time. At some point, I told her I liked her. But she was talking to the drummer during this period and saying 'I think he likes me, but I've been sort of trying to get rid of him.' The drummer was saying, 'Foreigners are not like Japanese people. You have to tell him straight up. If you want him to fuck off, you have to tell him to fuck off.' But then the drummer said, 'You haven't got many foreign friends. Why don't you just be friends with him?'"

"How did you communicate with her?"

"It was really hard. It was very mysterious, because somehow we were able to have really interesting conversations. The weird thing about language is that once you know the language, it's hard to remember a time when you didn't. When I was younger, I listened to Judy and Mary and didn't know what they were singing about. But now, when I listen to them I think, *of course, that's what the song is about.* It's the same thing with friends. I have a lot of friends who used to live in London. Now they live in Japan. We used to speak in English but now when we meet, we speak in Japanese. It doesn't feel weird, really. Japanese is just a language."

"How did you finally manage to convince her?"

"Through extreme force of willpower! I don't know... Persistence? I guess she just got used to me. We would go out every now and then. I was fairly forward and telling her that I liked her after the first month or so. It was because I was honest about it, maybe?"

"When did you feel that it was finally working?"

"At the time, we would go out somewhere and she'd come back to my place and then she would always go home. We'd never stayed at each other's house. But one day, she came around to my house and we kissed. She still went home after that, but I was like, 'Yes!'

"After, we would hang out a lot at each other's places. Especially, I would stay at her place, because I lived in a tiny apartment, whereas she lived closer to central Tokyo. I would stay at her place and go to work from there. We watched films and went to see friends' bands. We cooked for each other. Her parents had a restaurant and she was very much into food. She was playing music, so I would go and see her live shows."

"Why were you into her so much?"

"For one thing, she's a rock musician, but she's not like any other rock musician I know. Most rock musicians tend to be quite easy-going. She's definitely not easy-going! She's quite uptight. Most rock musicians love hanging out with other rock musicians and going to after-parties. She's not particularly into that either. She's much more focused on her career.

"I guess I found her a little bit mysterious and enigmatic. Also, a lot of rock musicians grew up listening to foreign music and they learned at least some English through that. They have an interest in overseas culture, because, for example, they want to know more about where Freddie Mercury came from. She isn't interested in overseas culture. She just listened to Japanese music, so she was like a typical Japanese person. It was like a puzzle to solve.

"We started living together within a year of being together. She's quite conservative. She's a little bit older than me. Her family has quite traditional Japanese viewpoints. So before we could move in together, I had to ask her parents' permission. That for me was incredibly nerve-wracking, because my Japanese still wasn't that great. She made me memorize the whole speech in perfect *keigo* (honorific language) about who I was, what job I did, how long I'd been in Japan, and my intentions towards their daughter. I was extremely nervous about it.

"We met her parents in an *izakaya* in Shinjuku. We walked into a Japanese-style room and they were there already. Straight away, her parents were so nice. No fucking problem! I was so nervous about this, because she'd built it up. Before I even had a chance to say all that stuff, they were asking all these questions. It was totally fine. We got drunk together and then I explained that we wanted to live together. They said, 'It's normal to get married first.' But I said, 'In Britain, we don't do that. We move in together and we see if we get on. And then you think about marriage.' They found it a little bit weird, but they said, 'Whatever. Fine. No problem.' That was that. We went apartment hunting and moved in about eleven months after we got together.

"We did a lot of stuff normal couples probably wouldn't do, because she was a musician. She didn't have any record label or management, although she did have a producer. She started working on her new album, so she needed help. I knew people because I had worked in the music industry. We would spend time doing that kind of thing. I went to her rehearsals. I took her fresh recordings to record labels. I helped her organize overseas tours.

"Within about a year of moving in, I proposed. I was twenty-nine then. It was quite an intense period. She was touring the States and our wedding was a week after. And we were having another wedding party in the UK. I was sleeping four hours a night, seven days a week.

"We went to Lake Kawaguchi, near Mount Fuji. It was the weekend before our birthdays and I decided to propose. I got a ring, though I managed to fuck up the size. In Japan, I think it's quite common that you propose and you choose the ring after. But in Britain, we don't do that. I had this brilliant idea of taking one of her rings. What I didn't think about was that she wore that ring on her middle finger! It was a different size.

"I got the ring, and I planned it all out. In Lake Kawaguchi, there was a shrine to the goddess of marriage. I thought that would be the place to do it. So I proposed there. She cried a bit and said, 'Yes.' I had to learn how to propose in Japanese.

"Man, going to wedding venues was so stressful! Getting married is so expensive. Wherever you go, you are looking at a couple of million yen (tens of thousands of dollars) at least. If you go to those places, they try to be as polite as possible because they want your money. They use super, super polite *keigo*. *Keigo* is so hard that even some Japanese people have trouble understanding it. I was absolutely out of my depth. I said to them, 'Sorry, would you mind being less polite?' But they couldn't because they all had bosses watching them. So a lot of it fell to my wife to either translate into normal Japanese for me, or to arrange it herself. In England, when you get married, your parents do most of the work. And they pay for it too, whereas we had to do everything ourselves while we were getting ready to go on a tour in the States.

"My parents were coming from England. Usually in Japan, most people get married in a sort of a church. It's 'western style.' But coming from a Jewish family, I couldn't get married in a fake church with a massive cross. So we went for a Japanese-style one. We had a ceremony at Asakusa Shrine. We chose the end of March because that's when the cherry blossoms were blooming. It would be nice to have the cherry blossoms around on our anniversary. Unfortunately, the cherry blossom bloomed late that year.

"I was incredibly stressed. We say, 'Let's never get divorced 'cause we don't want to go through the same stuff again!'"

His wife having a baby wasn't an easy process for Charles.

"I think for a man you never really feel like you are quite ready to have a baby. But it kind of got to a point where I thought it was now or never, especially because she was older. And then the earthquake happened. There was all the radiation stuff, and generally the news in those days was so gloomy. It wasn't a good time to have a baby, so we kind of put it off for a couple of months.

"Having a kid in a mixed-cultural relationship, there were so many things you hadn't even considered, like coming up with a name. We had so many long conversations and arguments over names. We didn't know if it was going to be a boy or a girl because we decided to wait to find out. We wanted to think of a name that could be pronounced exactly the same in English and Japanese. There aren't many names like that. You have names that are close like Risa or Lisa, but not quite the same. And trying to think of *kanji*! You've got to make sure that the number of strokes doesn't have a negative meaning. My *kanji* was terrible. I wasn't much help so she had to think about a lot of this stuff herself. There was a lot of paperwork, just like getting married. My Japanese wasn't quite good enough for that either.

"And choosing a hospital! Again, in England, you already have your GP who is like a family doctor. Any time for any problem, you go to them first and they say, 'OK, you see this kind of doctor next and come back to me.' In Japan you don't really have that. When you are having a kid, you have to choose a hospital by researching online. A lot of information out there was only in Japanese, so I was a bit useless. She would get very stressed out having to do all of that herself.

"In England, it's completely normal to have an epidural, which is like a knockout drug. You are awake, but you can't feel anything. But in Japan, most people have a natural birth. In England, even if you had a natural birth, it's never a hundred percent natural because they at least give you gas. It would be unthinkable to have a completely natural birth, whereas here, it seems the way to bond with your baby. I was begging her, 'Please, get an epidural. It's expensive here, but it's going to be horrible otherwise.'

"We were not able to get an epidural due to the schedule. Instead, we had something similar called *watsu-bunben* (pain-reducing drugs) that were available without reservation. But they were really useless, a huge waste of money.

"Then, when the baby was born, she had a very long labor. My daughter was just a little bit on the big side. She wouldn't come out. The labor was something like thirty-seven hours. Then the hospital managed to mess up and my wife had an infection in the wound. She ended up staying in the hospital for two weeks. And again, it's so frustrating when your Japanese isn't quite good enough. I have no problem with Japanese in day-to-day life, but medical terms, I had to learn all that stuff.

"As for me, I want her to grow up bilingual and bicultural. For a kid, that's a lot of pressure, I think. Already, she's two and speaks pretty much fifty-fifty English and Japanese, but her sentence structure is better in Japanese because she spends all day with my wife. She knows the Japanese and English words for some things, and she uses the Japanese words with my wife and English words with me. It's just completely natural without us teaching. I don't really feel worried about her learning.

"The thing is, the Japanese education system isn't very highly regarded overseas. I'd rather she got a Western education. Not an American education, because, for one thing, I don't want her to pick up an American accent!

"It's important to me, because if she ever moves to England, I want her to have a British accent. It's different. The spellings are different. If she went to a Japanese school, they would teach American English. That bugs me. So I think we've more or less settled on this British school in Tokyo. They use the British curriculum and they are highly rated. There are a few downsides. It's incredibly expensive, and there's also the turnover. A lot of the families work for just a few years in Japan and then leave.

"But basically, we've heard so many people's opinions including those of friends who went to international schools. Anyone who has any kind of foreign background at all says international school. Japanese people tend to say Japanese school. So it's really hard. I hated school. I'm naturally quite bright, but I hated studying. But I want to make sure she's happy whatever school she goes to."

Discussions

I really wanted to include Charles in this book because I think he overcame several layers of cultural barriers. His wife wasn't interested in Western culture or learning English, which I think made things quite hard for him. Despite that, Charles ended up dating her "through extreme force of willpower," and later married her.

One of the cultural issues in this story is the use of an epidural. As Charles pointed out, natural birth is much more popular in Japan. Some people think that experiencing the pain of birth is an important part of becoming a mother and a way of cultivating affection for your children. There are also other factors such as a lack of anesthesiologists at obstetric hospitals and insufficient insurance coverage. As a consequence, it's not always easy to get an epidural during childbirth, even if you want one.

Another cultural observation is that in Japan, American English is considered the standard, though the majority of Japanese people don't really know the differences between different types of English. In fact, when Japanese people talk about "overseas" (*kaigai*), they often mean the US. Japanese society in general has a lot of US influence.

3. Tomoko—What? Did I say I love you?

Mixed dating in Japan from a Japanese girl's perspective

TOMOKO USED TO DATE A Japanese guy. She wanted to break up with him, but she wasn't sure how to tell him.

Her boyfriend lived in another prefecture, but close enough to take the train to see her during the day. One day, she got a call from him at three in the morning. He wanted to talk to her but she wanted to sleep, so she hung up and went back to bed.

The next morning, when she woke up, she realized that someone was standing in front of her house. She looked out the door and saw her boyfriend standing there. *How is this possible?*, she thought. He lived more than 40 kilometers (25 miles) away. There was no train at night and he didn't have a car. He didn't even have a bike.

"I ran," he said.

That was just one story.

Tomoko is by no means the average Japanese girl. When she was nine, she moved to the US and spent two years there. After she came back to Japan, she went to an American school. On top of having an interesting upbringing, she is bisexual.

"I was really negative until I went to the US," she said. "I was reading books all day. I was even taking picture books to read at school. I didn't have a lot of friends. I was just not friendly. But after I moved to the US, I was forced to be positive.

"At first, I was kind of annoyed because I couldn't speak English at all. But the school put me into the ESL class, so I started learning English. After one year, I moved to the normal class. It took me one year to fit into the American culture. But after I got used to it, I had a really good life there."

When she returned to Japan, her parents enrolled her into an international school.

"Did you have many friends there?"

"Yes, I did. The atmosphere was good. Everyone had lived overseas, so there was no teasing even though I hadn't attended a normal Japanese school. There were cultural differences because some people were from other Asian countries. Others were from Europe and different places. But we had something in common, which was the experience of living overseas. If I had gone to a normal Japanese school, I think I would have been treated differently."

Japanese schools tend to be extremely homogeneous. Children with different backgrounds often become subjects of teasing and bullying.

"I graduated from the international school and got into a normal Japanese college in Kyoto. Those years were the worst of my life. Suddenly I couldn't fit into the culture.

"The very first girl I dated was when we were in the third year of junior high school. I was fifteen. We were both in the volleyball club and our club had a locker room. One day, I went there to change my clothes. She was also in the room. Suddenly, she kissed me and told me she loved me. That was the beginning of our relationship. She was Japanese, but she'd lived in Singapore.

"But we were too young, and it was over after a month or so. She realized that she liked boys more than girls."

"How did she know that you were interested in girls?"

"I think she didn't know. She just kissed me."

The first crazy boyfriend

"He was a friend of a friend. When my friend introduced him to me, he looked very Japanese. He suffered from depression, and he quit high school two weeks after we started our relationship. When he started to work as a truck driver, he became crazier and crazier. I was afraid of him, so I tried to stay away from him. But then, he got even crazier.

"He was free during the day because he didn't have school, and most of his shifts were at night. One day, he came all the way to my high school when I was taking a class. He opened the door, came in and said, 'Where's Tomoko?' My teacher was surprised and took us both to the teachers' office. She tried to calm him down, but she didn't succeed. His crazy behavior continued for three months.

"Once, he visited my *kendo* class in the gym. After a while, his mother noticed the crazy things he was doing, so they moved away."

The good girl

"My next relationship was with a girl who was my classmate. I think that was the longest relationship in my life. It was right after I broke up with the crazy boy. She was very pretty and she was a good girl. She was studying music and so was I, so we had a lot to talk about. I think it was me who said 'I love you.' But I think I loved her too much. I wanted to be with her as much as I could. She was busy because she had club activities, and she was trying to get into a very difficult university. I kept emailing and calling her. I think she was annoyed.

"It lasted two years. Then, she told me she couldn't handle me anymore, because I was going too far. I told her I didn't want to break up. But she had already made up her mind. So we broke up.

"I couldn't forget her for five years. She knew that, so she tried to avoid me. After high school, I couldn't contact her and that was so sad."

"Did you do anything crazy like your ex-boyfriend?"

"No! Well, I called her ten times a day. But I wasn't as crazy as my exes. I had common sense. That experience was awkward, because for a long time afterwards, even when I had boyfriends and girlfriends, I wasn't able to forget her."

The runner

"The next one was in college. We were in law school and that was the most demanding school in my university. But he was not as smart as the other students. He was kind of depressed because he couldn't get good grades in his first year.

"When we met, I was visiting my professor to talk about which graduate school I should go. He was also there to talk about the problems he was having with his courses. The classes were too difficult for him.

"We started talking. After we met several times, he told me he loved me. I think I still loved my ex-girlfriend, but we got together. He was not crazy the first month. We were a normal couple.

"After a month, I told him I couldn't be with him. It was too much because I wanted to study to get into graduate school. When I said that, his reaction was like, 'Oh, graduate school is more important than me?' Then he started acting crazy. Sometimes, I ignored his phone calls because he called me like forty times a day.

"One day, when I was sleeping, I got a phone call from him. He told me that if I didn't talk to him, he would come to my house. But it was like three in the morning, so I thought that was impossible. He lived in Kyoto and I lived in Nara. The distance was about 40 kilometers (25 miles). I just put away my phone and went back to sleep.

"When I woke up, it was six am. I went out to get my newspaper. But when I opened my door, somebody was there. I thought, *what? Who is it?* I looked more closely and it was my boyfriend. I asked, 'How did you come here? There's no train.' And he said, 'Oh, I ran.'"

"Didn't he have a bike or something?"

"I guess not, because he lived by himself and wasn't rich. He came from a poor family and had to support himself. I couldn't believe what he'd done. I told him that I didn't want anybody stalking me. He was shocked, and we started arguing in front of the door. Then my mom woke up and came outside. She was also surprised but she was actually glad that I had a boyfriend, because my mom wanted me to get married soon."

Her mom is a very traditional woman. She is very Japanese in many ways. When they were moving to the US, she didn't want to go at first, because she didn't think she would fit into American culture.

She was so "traditional" that she didn't think it was necessary for women to go to university. She even hesitated to pay for Tomoko's university (in Japan, it's usual for parents to pay the university tuition, and scholarships aren't widely available).

"I noticed that my boyfriend was just like my crazy ex-boyfriend, so I tried to keep a distance from him both physically and mentally. I tried to reduce the number of phone calls between us and the time we spent together. But the more I avoided him, the crazier he got. I wanted to break up, but I couldn't because he was acting too weird. I was only nineteen and I didn't know how to communicate with him effectively.

"Fortunately, after eight months, I applied to a domestic exchange program to a university in Tokyo. He was also thinking of studying abroad in Canada. So he went to Canada, and I thought, *this is my chance*. I deleted everything related to him, like phone numbers and Facebook. That was how it ended.

"I don't know why people become that weird. Once, after he went to Canada and I deleted everything, he sent some airmail to me. He said he would give up studying abroad and come to Japan. I think he also had a mental illness, but he wasn't aware of it. But the good thing was that he didn't send me any more letters.

"I was just sad. He was kind in many ways, because he loved me so much. It's not good to say this, but he was very obedient to me. For example, if I had said, 'Go buy me some clothes,' he would have done that. I mean, I didn't do that, but he was like that.

"He mostly loved to watch movies. He lived in Kyoto so we went to see temples and shrines. Sometimes we just went to a music studio because he played the guitar. I think dating was normal."

The smart guy

"The next one was an American guy but unfortunately, I don't remember a lot about him. We didn't see each other many times because he lived in Gunma and I was in Tokyo. He was an English teacher at an elementary school. A friend introduced him to me. He didn't speak Japanese. I think he was really interested in dating Japanese girls because he loved Japan. I was also interested in dating internationally.

"He was really smart. He graduated from Berkeley. I think he majored in chemical science, but he was an English teacher. I couldn't catch what he said sometimes, because the things he talked about were too difficult for me. So I thought I couldn't be with him, because I wasn't as smart as him. Also, I had a plan to go overseas. I told him I wanted to break up, and he just accepted it.

"He was not crazy. He hadn't done anything like stalking. And he didn't act like he was the best thing in the world, like my ex-husband."

The Taiwanese guy

"After I broke up with the American guy, I went to Taiwan. I taught English at a really poor school in a rural place. Everyone was curious about me because I was Japanese. They'd never seen a foreigner before. At first they were very kind, but then they noticed I didn't speak Chinese at all. They started becoming distant. I had nobody to help me. I was lonely and it was so difficult because I didn't know the language.

"There was one young man who was a soldier. He couldn't speak English well, but he could understand it. So when I needed something or wanted to go somewhere, I would talk to him. He had a car and he drove me to supermarkets. I started to think about him a lot, and he also started to think about me.

"But he quit being a soldier after two months. I became lonely again. I was kind of depressed because nobody spoke English and I couldn't speak Japanese for two months. I was completely isolated. The kids played with me and they made me happy, but there was no real conversation.

"Then the soldier guy contacted me on Facebook. He texted me, 'Are you OK?' He lived somewhere else now, but it wasn't that far. I applied for a week's absence and we traveled through Taiwan. I didn't think it was good to travel with a guy I wasn't in a relationship with, but I was so lonely and sad. Later on, he told me that he wanted to tell me he loved me, but he was scared.

"I came back to the village and he started talking to me on Facebook a lot. When my classes finished at three or four, I went to play with the kids and then I went back to my dorm at six. Then I went on Facebook and talked to him. That was kind of fun, even if it was on the Internet.

"Several days before I went back to Japan, we went on another trip and he took me to Taipei. He told me he loved me. First, I thought it would be difficult because I was going back to Japan. But I was so sad for him because he had done a lot of things for me. I couldn't have lived without him. So I said OK.

"I went back to Japan. I was kind of busy preparing for the entrance exam for graduate school. He told me that he felt sad because we couldn't have private Skype calls. I took the exam for the graduate school in August and I passed. He said he was coming to Japan in September.

"He came to Japan, but he told me that he hadn't booked a hotel. He was thinking he could stay at my house. But I was living with my parents. I said, 'Just go to a love hotel (a short-stay hotel for couples, often a cheap option for staying overnight),' which he did. I needed to go to school the next day, but I skipped my classes and went to the library to book a proper hotel for him. I searched for a hotel all day.

"He stayed one week and went back to Taiwan. There was one crazy thing: he didn't bring a condom. Sex education in Taiwan is probably the worst among developed countries. He didn't even think of it. The crazier thing was, he still wanted to have sex.

"I told him that I would get pregnant if he didn't use a condom. He asked, 'What's the problem with having a baby?' I said, 'What? Are you going to marry me if I have a baby?' He said, 'Yes, why not?' I think he was in a rush because he was turning thirty. Taiwan is traditional, so his parents wanted him to get married soon. He had a brother and sister who were both married, and he was the only one who wasn't married yet. I actually began to suspect he started a relationship with me because he wanted to get married.

"I told him I wasn't going to have sex with anybody who didn't have a condom. I forced him to say he would go and buy one at a convenience store. But the next day, when I met him after school, he still hadn't bought a condom. I asked him why. He said, 'Because I can't speak Japanese.' He was afraid to go to a convenience store! He'd never been overseas before. He didn't have experience in a country that was completely different from his.

"We didn't have sex until he came to Japan. He had had only one relationship before. He said that it lasted for eight years, but he only had sex with her once. That was strange. I don't even know if it's true or not.

"He went back to Taiwan after a week. I was kind of irritated, because he wasn't a brave guy and he wasn't responsible about sexual stuff. But I didn't want to give this relationship up, so I just continued.

"I spent one more month without seeing him. At the time, he didn't have a job. He wanted to be a teacher, but becoming a teacher in Taiwan is really difficult because, like Japan, they don't have many children. He had failed the test more than ten times. We were both stressed. Sometimes, I couldn't understand his culture and he couldn't understand mine. We started to argue.

"One day, we had such a big argument on Skype that I told him we were going to break up. He was like 'What?' and he just shut down Skype. Three days later, he called and told me he was in Japan. He said, 'I'm at Itami (the Osaka International Airport).' I was like, 'Huh?'

"I skipped school and went to the airport. He was there. He said, 'I wanted to see you.' And again, he hadn't booked a hotel! So I had to book a hotel for him again. Oh, by the way, he didn't bring a condom either.

"I couldn't just let him go back to Taiwan, so we stayed in the hotel together. But my parents were getting suspicious because I was out for five days. They called and asked me what I was doing. I had told them that my friend from Taiwan was visiting, but I hadn't said he was a boy.

"They noticed little by little. They called me and asked me, 'Are you with a boy?' I said no, but they were very suspicious. I told him that I needed to go back home and then come back to the hotel. Then he started to cry.

"You know, he was thirty years old. I told him that I would go back to my house and come back to the hotel by bike. It was nine pm and there wouldn't be any trains later. The hotel was in Nara so I thought it would be close to my house. I went back to my house and waited until my parents fell asleep, then I went outside and took my brother's bike. When I left my house, it was two am.

"It took me three hours to get to the hotel. When I arrived at the hotel, it was five am. He was still waiting, but I was very tired. I tried to stay awake but I almost fainted. That was the last day of his visit. He didn't wake me up when he left. He went to the airport and went back to Taiwan. When I woke up, it was eight am. I rode the bike all the way home again.

"When I turned on Skype, he was already in Taiwan. He shouted at me, 'Why did you sleep even though I was there!?' I was so confused because I'd done all this for him. I realized I couldn't marry him. And I didn't want to waste his time, because he needed to find someone else. So I told him I wanted to break up with him. At first, he was so upset. He shut down Skype again. But several hours later, he called me. He was crying.

"That was when he started to comment a lot on my Facebook. It was so crazy."

He commented on pretty much every single Facebook status update she made. He would say, "I love you so much. I still want to be with you," regardless of the content of her status.

"But I just couldn't break up with him, because I still appreciated all of the things he had done in Taiwan. I tried to be friends with him but I couldn't. I thought maybe I should find a new boyfriend because then he would give up.

"That was when I met my ex-husband."

The ex-husband

"It was after I got into the graduate school in Tokyo. I was studying international relations and I had an opportunity to visit a US Army base. They needed me to translate some stuff. I met some Army people and my ex-husband was among them.

"After I finished my translation, I had a chance to look around the base. He was the one who showed me around. After that, he asked for my phone number. He told me that he wanted to know more about Japan. I thought I shouldn't give him my number. But I was afraid because he was in the Army.

"I just gave him my email address. He started emailing me. After a month, he suddenly said he wanted to be in a relationship with me."

"But I wasn't sure. I thought I needed to be careful, because I had already met a lot of crazy guys. So I said, 'Maybe we should be friends first.' I told him we couldn't go on a date but just a friendly meeting. Two months passed, and he told me again that he wanted to be in a relationship. I thought he was a good guy, so it would be OK.

"At the time, I was kind of unstable because of the big Tohoku earthquake in Japan. I wasn't used to earthquakes, so my body was feeling weird. It was shaking sometimes. It was some kind of illness."

It is widely known that some people develop PTSD-like symptoms after viewing media images of natural disasters or violent events. After the earthquake in 2011, some Japanese people were reported to have these symptoms.

"When I sat in front on a computer, I felt like my body was shaking. But I was a graduate student and I needed to use a computer a lot. It was so aggravating. I didn't feel like studying, so I got into a relationship with my ex-husband. It was interesting at first because he took me to the base and to American parties. That was something I wouldn't have experienced without him.

"After several weeks, he told me he wanted to marry me. It was so fast. He was twenty-eight and I was still twenty-three or twenty-four. At first, I said no. But he told me he wanted to get married now. It was because he was about to leave the Army. It was not his decision. I think he'd done something crazy.

"I couldn't decide things in my normal way, because I wasn't stable at the time. Another reason was that my Taiwanese ex-boyfriend was still stalking me. He just couldn't give up. I was so irritated. So I had this bad idea that if I married the American guy, maybe it would stop. I still thought it was too fast, but I got married anyway.

"Two days after we got married, he told me he had gotten kicked out of the Army and he was going back to the States. But the worst thing was that he had a child with his ex-wife and he hadn't told me about that as well. I asked him why he was going back to the States. I mean, he could stay a few more months in Japan and find a job. Then he said he wanted to go back to see his child. What? I didn't know he had a kid!

"I started to suspect that he might be a crazy guy too. I said, 'Hey, it's only been two days since we got married and this is already happening. If you act crazy, I don't want this anymore.' He started apologizing. He said, 'I'm very sorry, but it's very difficult to get a job in Japan since I don't speak Japanese. I'll try to come back to Japan again.' I accepted that, because it was the only choice I had.

"I was still a student in Tokyo. I was really stressed. My husband wasn't in Japan and he didn't have a job. We had no money. But he said, 'Could you please send me money? Could you please support me financially?' I was thinking, *I am a student. How can I do that?*

"I needed to get a job, so I decided to take a break from school. He had been asking me to come over to the States, but I didn't have money. I started working as a rickshaw driver because the pay was so good. I worked for six months and made enough money to go to the States. I bought the ticket and went to Louisiana where he lived.

"He had been living with his parents, but he moved to his cousin's house because I was coming. It was kind of a temporary share house. His cousin was a good guy. He was engaged to a white woman who was beautiful and very kind. She took me to nice places around. But she told me it was a really bad decision to marry my ex-husband. She said, 'You need to get divorced.' Her fiancé also told me that I shouldn't be with him.

"They told me that my ex-husband was not independent enough. He loved video games and gambling, the only fun things he could do in Louisiana. I met his mother. I was surprised that she had been divorced three times.

"I came back to Japan and told him we needed to get divorced. He got really upset. He shouted and swore a lot on Skype. He said his cousin's fiancée was a bitch. I didn't agree. I told him, 'You are more of a bitch than her!'

"He thinks he's smart. That's the worst thing about him. He always said he could be a doctor. He never went to a university. He only graduated from a military high school. He's not smart at all. He's like a really typical, overconfident guy."

"How long did you live in the US?"

"It was about two months. I was married for a year in total. When I said I wanted a divorce, it was like six months after I got married. Six months was still too long. I should've gotten a divorce right away.

"He was really angry, but he said OK in the end. We needed to get divorced in Japan because we had gotten married in Japan. But he couldn't figure out how to gather all the documents. I told him everything we needed and I even prepared the application form for him. I sent it to the US, but he didn't send it back for four months. I asked him about that a lot on Facebook or Skype. But he didn't respond. Finally, after four months, he sent it back to me, but he hadn't filled out the application correctly. I got a new form, and I sent it to the US again. He didn't send it back for another two months. So technically, we were married for one year.

"I finally got divorced in November 2012. One month later, he told me he was with another Japanese woman and she was pregnant. He wanted a divorce certificate. I needed to find a lawyer to make that document and it would cost me around 100,000 yen (about $1,000). I told him I wasn't going to pay for that. He said, 'Why can't you find the money!? I'm having a baby!' And I was wondering, *why on earth did his girlfriend decide to have a baby with this guy?* I heard his girlfriend was from Hokkaido (a northern island about the size of Ireland). I checked her Facebook profile. She was in Japan waiting to get together with him so I think it was long distance. I thought about contacting her, but I just didn't want to get involved in their problems anymore.

"I wanted the divorce certificate for a cheap price, and needed to hire a lawyer. I contacted a Japanese girl from my high school who was working for a lawyer. She introduced me to him. He was really nice, and he said he only wanted 20,000 yen (about $200).

"I prepared a divorce certificate and I sent it to the US. I was like, 'Finally, no more contact!' I have no idea what he is doing now."

The Navy guy

"I met this guy at a Navy party. My friend from the Army took me there. My friend was my ex-husband's friend and he was not crazy. We had a bingo party and I won a PS3. But I didn't want it, because I didn't play video games. A Navy guy said he would buy it from me. We started talking. I was really stressed about my ex-husband and asked him, 'What should I do?' He gave me a lot of advice about international laws and explained how the American marriage system worked.

"We were friends for three months. Then he was being deployed to South Asia. He told me that when he came back, he wanted to be in a relationship with me. I said, 'We'll think about it.'

"So he went on deployment and came back to Japan. He contacted me asking, 'Are you still interested in me?' I thought he was an interesting guy, because he knew all the laws and a lot about American security systems, and I was studying international relations. I said, 'OK, maybe we can be in a relationship without any sexual stuff.'"

Tomoko generally prefers girls to guys. She says she doesn't have much to do when she has sex with men, because she prefers women's bodies.

"We started being in a relationship. I only had sex with him once. That was around the time when North Korea dropped a bomb on South Korea and he said he needed to go back to the States. So I went to his house and… that was the first and the last time we had sex."

"Did he have a condom?"

"Yes, of course!"

The Osakan girl

"I wasn't doing well at graduate school. So I quit school and started looking for a job. It was tricky because I didn't have any experience.

"I was just staying home and getting more and more depressed. The girl who introduced me to the lawyer contacted me and said, 'Are you OK?' I said, 'Well, I'm not well.' She said, 'We can have dinner together and talk.' She told me she had just broken up with her Taiwanese boyfriend and couldn't forget him. I gave her some advice because I had a similar experience. We started talking a lot on Facebook.

"One day—it was after meeting her several times—I was so drunk. I went back home, turned on Skype, and called her. I told her I wanted to be in a relationship with her, when I didn't really. She was angry. She was like, 'You're just joking, right?' I was like, 'No, I'm not joking.' But she shut down Skype and I went to sleep.

"The next day, she messaged me and said, 'Is it true what you said last night?' I was like, 'Uh, what did I say?' I didn't remember. She got angry again. She said, 'You are the kind of person who says "I love you" to anybody!' I said, 'Did I say "I love you" to you?' She was so angry, and she stopped talking to me for about a week. I kept sending her messages saying, 'Sorry, sorry, sorry.'

"She saw the message and said, 'I can be in a relationship with you if you can honestly say you love me.' I was confused because I didn't know that she also liked girls. So I asked her if she was a lesbian and she said, 'No. But I love you because you are you.' I wasn't convinced, because the people I was in relationships with always turned out to be weird later on. I told her, 'Maybe you need to think about it a little bit.' I was still in a relationship with the American guy. So she said OK.

"But after she told me she loved me, I think I had a crush on her. I made up my mind and said goodbye to the American guy. I called him on Skype and told him. He was back in his home country. He was like, 'You like women? I didn't know that.' But actually, I had told him before. He just forgot. His answer was, 'Oh, I can have sex with two girls.' I sighed and quit Skype.

"He was OK with the breakup at first, but as time passed by, he said he didn't want to break up. He started to call and text me a lot. I told him not to do it. Then he became crazier and crazier like my previous boyfriends. But I wasn't afraid anymore, because he was far away.

"I was still in Tokyo, but my girlfriend was in Osaka. So I went back to my parents' house in Nara, which was very close to Osaka. We had a lot of time to date. We were happy with each other.

"I found a job there, but the pay was really bad. I needed to find a better job. The job hunting went quite well. I got an offer from a foreign company, which was good because I could use my English and Chinese language skills. The problem was that the company was in Tokyo. I told her that I needed to go back to Tokyo again. She wasn't happy. She was planning to live with me. She cried a lot, but I told her that it was an important decision. She accepted it and I came to Tokyo again.

"Meanwhile, the American guy kept emailing me, but I was ignoring him. I didn't tell him my new address in Tokyo. Once, he said he was going to my parents' house. I said, 'Please don't do that! If you do that, I'm going to kill myself.' He was shocked, so he didn't try.

"I don't know how he got my new address—I think some of his friends told him—but one day, after I finished my job and went back to my house, I found him in front of my house. He came all the way to Japan uninvited just to see me.

"I went to the police. I was afraid he might have a gun because he was in the Navy. Police officers came back to my house with me. Then we talked. It was like déjà vu, because he hadn't booked a hotel! The police officers helped me look for a hotel. I told him, 'If you come near my company or my house again, I will take you to the police station.' I think he spent time in Japan on his own after that before going back to the States, but I'm not sure, because I never saw him again."

◄ ♥ ►

Tomoko wants to marry her girlfriend.

"Now, I'm stable with my girlfriend. I really want to get married, but I can't do that in Japan. And it's not a good idea to go overseas now, because I just started working for my company. So I am thinking of adopting her. My birthday is in July and she was born in October. She is younger than me, so technically, I can be her mother. We can legally be a family. Because she works for a lawyer, she asked him about it. He said he could help us."

It's possible in Japan for adults to legally adopt other adults. Although this is usually used by childless people to pass their assets or a family business on to their chosen successor, it's also a loophole used by many same-sex couples to enjoy the legal benefits of being family.

"What kind of person is she?"

"She's very quiet. She's loud only when she drinks. She is a dancer and performs in Osaka. So I watch her shows sometimes. She is also into social dancing, but I'm such a bad dancer.

"Sometimes she comes to my house in Tokyo. When I go to Kansai, I can't stay at her house because she still lives with her parents. But from October she is going to live by herself, so I think I can stay at her apartment."

"What do you love about her?"

"Maybe, one thing is that she is a girl. She's not like me. She's so girly. She's beautiful, not only on the outside, but also from the inside. She's quiet, but it's good because I don't want any more aggressive people in my life. I like to talk and she likes to listen to my stories and... it's a good match. She doesn't restrict me too much either."

"And she's not crazy?"

"No, not yet."

Discussions

One can't help but notice a pattern in Tomoko's relationships: the guys she dates tend to be very obsessive. But the important thing here is that it happens regardless of their nationalities. She has had Japanese, Taiwanese, and American boyfriends, and most of them turned out to be obsessive. So, I think it is safe to say that it's not something cultural.

Tomoko says a possible reason for this is that she is too kind. She doesn't want to say no. Knowing her, this makes sense to me and there is one episode that I am reminded of.

Once, I went out to a club with Tomoko. A guy approached her and started talking. I didn't have any problem with that, because she was just a friend. But when the guy started trying to kiss her, it occurred to me that she didn't actually want to interact with him at all. I stepped in and chased the guy away. She said, "Why didn't you help me earlier?" But from my perspective, she wasn't clear about her intentions. There were a lot of things she could have done. For example, she could have excused herself and left.

The thing is, she seems happier with girls than with guys. She says that she prefers girls herself. Now that she is with a girl, she seems happy. I hope this one will work out well for her.

4. Joshua—My friend said, "Don't tell her I'm from Africa"

How an African guy's dating experience is different from others

COMING TO JAPAN MUST HAVE been quite a challenge for Joshua. He is from Kenya. Before he came to go to university, he had little knowledge about the country.

"I didn't know a lot about Japan," he said. "I knew a little bit because of electronics, which I liked. I knew Toyota was from Nagoya. I used to watch NHK World. You can watch that in Kenya, but they only talk about sumo. So in the sumo seasons, I used to see very huge people. I wasn't really fascinated by the culture. I applied to study in Japan because of its advanced technologies."

Joshua seemed quite popular in Kenya. Part of the reason is that he was a smart kid and won a prize in a math contest, making him bit of a regional celebrity. When he mentioned his name, girls would recognize it.

"I had my first girlfriend in primary school. I was eleven and almost finished with school. I had an accident and broke my leg. When I was in the hospital, they told me I needed somebody to help me get back to my normal life. There were people who specialized in doing that. So I was living with this person. They had a daughter. I didn't have the courage to talk to her, but a guy introduced me to her. She kind of liked me back.

"That was the first time I had sex. She said, 'Hey, my grandma is away. Do you want to come over?' So I stayed there for a night. She was more experienced than I was. I think she had had sex before. She was the same age as me, but two years behind in school.

"But I was finishing primary school. I was thinking, *I'm a high school student, but she is still in primary school. I don't think I can do this anymore.* So I broke up with her.

"The second year in high school, I had my second girlfriend. It was silly. We were communicating by sending letters."

"Do you mean snail mail?"

"Yeah. I was in a boys' boarding school, and she was in a girls' boarding girl school. In boarding school, you couldn't go out unless you had a very good reason. Phones were not allowed in school. There were strict rules. No phones. No radios. No TV.

"Writing letters was a lot of fun. You know, you like opening them when they arrive. And you try adding some good vocabulary to show off how good you are. People would use dictionaries to find difficult words and idioms. I used it to impress my girlfriends. But it was also a way of improving your vocabulary."

"In what language did you write?"

"English was the medium of communication. In Kenya, there are many tribes. When I speak to someone from my own tribe, I speak my tribe's language, but in high school, the language you use to communicate is mostly English. Teachers teach in English and talk to you in English. When you talk to somebody educated or when you have an intellectual conversation, you use English."

"Did your second girlfriend write well?"

"I don't know. Her writing was not really perfect. I would read her letter and think, *it's not good*. When I was in the third year, we broke up, mostly because of her English. I was smarter than she was. We had this thing called 'booting.' To boot someone, you write a booting letter telling her you are not going to be her boyfriend anymore.

"I think the difference in Japan is that Japanese people care a lot about how good your accent is. That's what makes people think that you speak good English. But there are many types of English in the world. English in Kenya is different from English in Uganda, but it's still English. It's not based on your accent. It's based on how well you use vocabulary and grammar.

"I met another girl at an 'outing.' An outing is where you get to meet girls from other high schools. It can be a sports event, or a science or music competition. It was official, but for students, you would go there to meet girls."

"How did you approach girls?"

"Sometimes you'd have a friend who came with his friends from primary school and he introduces you. Or your friend would say, 'I dare you to approach that girl!' Then you just go and introduce yourself. You need a lot of courage to do that. The school you are from is also very important. My school was a really good school, so girls would think, *Oh, he is from a better high school!* I was very smart in math. I was in the top three in the contest, but I was the best in math in the whole school. We had a national math contest, so they heard about me on the radio.

"That's how I met the third girl. She kind of knew me already. When I told her my name, she said, 'Oh yeah. I've heard of you.'

"After high school, I went to Nairobi. Then I came back, and got a job because I had really good grades. In Kenya, if you are going to a public university, you have to wait for two years to be able to get into the university.

"I was teaching math. By that time, writing letters wasn't fun anymore, because I had finished high school. My third girlfriend was happy being with me because I was from a better high school. But I ended up not communicating.

"She was a good writer. I liked her. She was really nice. We became friends again, and I was thinking about marrying her sometime."

After that, he dated one girl seriously. However, he then got a scholarship to study at a Japanese university and decided to come to Japan. The girl stayed behind in Kenya.

The Skype girl

The first place he lived in in Japan was Osaka. He was there for three years, going to a language school.

"My school was only for foreign students. We used to have events where Japanese people came and interacted with us. It was like a culture fair. There was food, cultural stuff, music, and dancing. I met one of my first girlfriends there. She was eighteen and I was nineteen. We dated for a while, but I was living in a place where there was a curfew. So we just went out for dinner. We ended up breaking up."

"Did you think that dating in Japan was different from dating in Kenya?"

"One of the differences is that in Kenya, when you go out with a girl, the guy usually pays for everything. In Japan, it's different. We would split the bill most of the time. She paid half, and I paid half.

"In Japan, many girls smoke. That's not common in Kenya. In Kenya, only high-end prostitutes smoke because they have to entertain men who smoke. So when I saw many Japanese girls smoking, I wondered, *is this what I think it is?*

"After my first girlfriend in Japan, I met another girl online. At that time, we had this thing called 'Skype Me.' If you are on Skype Me, anybody can talk to you. So, she contacted me. We ended up talking for a long time, and she gave me her number. She lived in Iwate (a northern prefecture) but we became sort of boyfriend and girlfriend online. I traveled there and stayed at her place for a week. She also came to my place after that. It was a long-distance relationship. But it suddenly ended.

"The thing is, she smoked. One time, I met her in Tokyo. We went to a restaurant together. She smoked and kissed me. I didn't like that. It was my first experience dating a girl who smoked. She kind of got pissed off because I didn't like her smoking. But she was also different from other Japanese girls. We went to Disneyland, and she kissed me in public. The other girlfriends I had were up for kissing when they were inside but not outside. I think it was because she had lived in Canada for two years and had had a Canadian boyfriend there.

"I met yet another girl through Skype Me. She was in Canada then, but we became friends. She was originally from Osaka. She had had a boyfriend who was from Cameroon. She was older than me. I was twenty-one and she was twenty-five or twenty-six.

"After she came back to Japan, we would go out to dinner but we didn't make it official. It was very casual. And we fought a lot. Mostly, it was because I was always late. I was five minutes or sometimes ten minutes late. She was very strict. When I left Osaka, we broke it off. We just remained friends.

"There was one other girl I loved very much. With other girls, I didn't think I could live with them or wanted to spend my life with them. But this one was different.

"She didn't like me back. She was studying Amharic in university. Amharic is an Ethiopian language. She was in liberal arts, but one of her classes was about Ethiopia. She wanted to meet someone from Africa, so a friend of mine introduced me to her. She was so beautiful that when I looked at her pictures, I would cover my eyes. We became friends and she Skyped me every night. There was a Japanese reggae artist called Spinna B-ill and one of his songs was called "Lion's Child." We would talk about it a lot. I liked her, but she said she just wanted to be friends.

"She is married to a Korean now. She lives in Korea. She went to Canada to study English and met a guy who'd also gone there to study English. When they came back, they started dating long distance and ended up getting married. She was the kind of girl that I would have loved to marry. She was down to earth and beautiful. Last year, she said, 'Hey, come and visit me!' But I didn't go."

Hip-hop girls

"Do you think girls in Osaka are more approachable than in Tokyo?"

"Exactly. Whenever I go to Osaka, I go to a club. Sometimes I meet girls, and I end up having a one-night stand. This happens in Osaka more than in Tokyo. In Tokyo, you talk to ten girls and you only get one. But in Osaka, the first three girls, you are going to succeed.

"But even in Osaka, I found dating really hard. I met two types of girls: the first were girls who were interested in Africa. Most of them were studying something to do with Africa in school. They end up meeting you and getting to know you. If you are a good guy, they will date you. These girls are interested in foreigners, but it doesn't matter where you are from.

"Then there were other girls who just wanted Americans. When you are in a club and you say you are from Kenya, they are not interested. Or if you are from a developing country, they are not interested. No Asians. No Indians. No Africans. There are also girls who specifically want African-Americans. They are usually into hip-hop. There are African guys who get girls because they dress hip-hop style. I don't really dress like that.

"I have some friends, mostly from Tanzania, who lie to girls that they are from the US. They get girls because girls think they are American. They try to change their accents so they sound more American, and many girls will fall for that. Once a friend of mine said to me, 'Hey, I'm meeting a girl and I told her I'm from the US. So don't tell her I'm from Tanzania.' I don't really care, because that's their life. But personally, I hate saying something like that. I like being Kenyan, and I want girls to like me because of my intelligence and my culture."

The high school teacher

After Osaka, he moved to Okayama to attend university. Okayama is a western prefecture right next to Hiroshima.

"Okayama was smaller, but there were actually many foreign students there. I think it was somewhere around the top ten in terms of the number of foreigners. The foreign community was very strong. We organized a lot of events.

There were two breeds of foreign students: exchange students, and masters or Ph.D. students. The exchange students were there for six months or one year, and most of them were from Europe. And the others were mostly Asians, Africans, or sometimes Americans.

"I went to an event where I was talking to guys from France, Sweden, and England. And then three more guys came and said 'Hi' and we were kind of mingling. When I said, 'I'm Joshua and I'm from Kenya,' these guys were like, 'Is Kenya Africa? I want to see animals!' and they moved on.

"It was really hard to date university girls in Okayama. Most of the exchange students had girlfriends, because the girls liked European or American culture. They didn't know anything about Africa.

"But when I went to a club, I got a woman sometimes. The only problem was that Okayama was small and the people who went clubbing were always the same. Once, I said to my friend, 'Hey, I had sex with this girl.' He asked me, 'What's her name?' I told him and he said, 'Yeah, I had sex with that girl last week.' It was a small pool. If you made a mistake, everybody would know it.

"But the second year, I ended up having a girlfriend. I was giving a presentation about my country. It was in Japanese, and there weren't many foreigners who spoke Japanese, so I got a lot of opportunities from television or radio shows. At the event, this girl came to me and said, 'Wow that was a nice presentation! I'd love to learn more about Kenya,' and gave me her number.

"That was the beginning of 2010. I was twenty-three then and she was thirty. She was a nice girl. She had really nice boobs and a nice ass. She was like, 'Let's hang out. I have a car. Let's go driving!' She told me she was a high school teacher. She'd lived in France for six years and she spoke really fluent French. But she was teaching English.

"She was different from other girls, because most girls liked taking *purikura* (instant photos taken in a photo booth, popular among teenage girls) or singing karaoke. She wasn't like that. We would stay at her house watching movies. We would choose one movie per weekend. The only problem was that her school was also in Okayama, so we couldn't hang out there, because she didn't want her students to see her. We had to go somewhere else."

"What language did you guys speak?"

"Japanese."

"Did you always speak Japanese with girls?"

"It depends on the girl. Most of the time, the girls I dated spoke English, but they realized that they couldn't explain a lot of stuff in English. And they knew that I spoke Japanese well so they didn't bother to speak English anymore. Sometimes, when that girl had problems with English, she would come to me.

"But the thing is, she was born and raised in Okayama. She had a sister, but her sister was married to a Japanese-Canadian guy and lived in Indonesia because of her husband's job. So, my girlfriend said, 'My parents are getting old and I'm the only child who is in Japan. I have the responsibility of taking care of my parents.' If she was going to marry someone, he would have to remain in Okayama. But I was just finishing university and going for a Ph.D. and after the Ph.D., I would have a lot of options. There was no way I would get a job in Okayama unless I could work in a university, but I didn't know if there was such an opportunity. So we broke up. We are still friends."

The friend of a friend

Then he came to Tokyo in 2011 for a Ph.D. program.

"I used to go to a club in Shibuya. They had a discount ticket only for foreigners. It was 1000 yen and all you can drink. It was so hard to talk to girls. I went to Roppongi but still, it wasn't easy.

"I was in Kobe two weeks ago at a small beach, swimming, walking around, and talking to random girls. They talk back to you! From there, you can ask their number. But in Tokyo, most of the time, you talk to them and they look at you, but they don't say anything. That's one thing about Tokyo that is different from Osaka. In Osaka, they will talk to you. When they see a black guy, they think they have to speak English or French. But when you say 'hi' in Japanese, they say, 'Oh, you speak Japanese?' And then they'll try to get to know you. They end up giving you their number very, very fast without you even asking.

"But I had some dates in Tokyo. The girl in Osaka who didn't like me back had a friend, and when I moved to Tokyo, the friend moved to Tokyo too. One thing led to another and we ended up having sex. We started dating. But I was going to school and I was busy.

"One day she said, 'Hey, one of my friends is coming from Cambodia to visit me.' But I didn't know her friend was a guy and staying at her place.

"I met her the following day. She had an iPhone and you know, you see the messages on the lock screen. The phone was near me and I saw the guy's message saying, 'It's good your period came.' I was wondering, *why is he talking about her period?* That's how I found out they had had sex. She met him in Cambodia and had dated him before. She said, 'If I had told you, you would have been angry about it.' I was so pissed off.

"In the end, I forgave her. She was sending messages and calling me all the time saying, 'I'm sorry.' I thought, *OK, what the heck.*

"Then she suddenly became serious. She said, 'Hey, I'm turning twenty-six and I want to get married. I think you are the one for me.' But she had cheated on me. I didn't like that. So I told her, 'You are great, but I'm sorry, I'm from Africa and in Africa, there's a lot of AIDS. If I take you home and you end up sleeping with someone else, and if you don't tell me and I sleep with you, you'll give me AIDS. I will be so scared. I don't think this is going to work out.'

"One thing I didn't like about her was that she was a typical Japanese girl. She had no boobs. I had bigger boobs than her. She was nice, but she wasn't that attractive to me.

"I broke up with her in 2012, but she kept coming to my place. She would come late at night. We continued having sex for a long time. She thought we were going to get back together.

"She actually ended up dating my best friend who was living in Osaka by then. But he didn't know I had dated her. When I came to Tokyo, we weren't really communicating. If he'd told me he was dating her, I would have told him.

"Actually, the girl told me not to tell him. The guy found out from another friend. The last time I heard from her, she was planning to move to Hiroshima. They were planning to get married. Maybe I'm not going to be invited to her wedding."

Joshua hasn't had a girlfriend since.

"That was basically my dating life. Since then, I've never had anything serious. Basically, most of the girls I meet can't speak English, but I speak really good Japanese. Very few foreigners do, so that's why I am sometimes successful with girls. A few months ago, I met two girls and one came to my place and we had sex, and it was like my birthday present. The other one gave me a blowjob in a restroom. She seemed crazy. I met her at one of these international parties. It was ten thirty and the party was going to end by eleven. She was there and I talked to her. Within a few minutes, she said, 'Take me out.'"

"What do you think of Japanese girls in bed?"

"They are not good in bed. They lie down and wait for you to do something. There was only one girl in Okayama who was really good in bed. She was active. The other girls I had in Japan didn't have any moves."

Discussions

Joshua said dating in Japan was difficult, but by Japanese standards, his dating life wasn't bad at all. He dated more than a few girls and had some extra sexual encounters. He is no less popular than the average Japanese guy.

One potentially controversial theme is the girls who were specifically interested in African-American guys. Many seem to be interested in hip-hop and other African-American music. For example, Amy Yamada, a Japanese writer, is quite open about her interest in African-American men and music, and African-American men are often featured in her stories.

When it comes to Africa, Japanese people tend to know very little about the continent. This makes it hard for Joshua to meet people who can see beyond the black and African stereotypes.

Another interesting observation he makes is that people are more approachable outside Tokyo. I have the same impression; I've been to about thirty countries around the world, but I would have to say people in Tokyo are exceptionally unapproachable. In Tokyo, people tend to be very cautious of strangers. If Tokyoites seem cold to you, you shouldn't take it personally.

5. Michelle—Then I checked his phone when he was sleeping

A story of a Finnish party girl

"**A**RE YOU A PARTY GIRL?" I asked Michelle.

"Yeah, I guess," she said. My memories of her are always associated with parties. At those parties, I would always go home before the last train. She would always stay.

The first time I met her, it was at a *hanami party*, a Japanese-style picnic in the cherry blossom season. Blonde and petite, Michelle was the kind of girl many Asian guys would be into. In addition, she spoke fluent Japanese.

She was born in Finland and grew up there. At fifteen, she moved to Singapore and went to an international school for a few years. After finishing high school in Finland, she moved to Japan.

"Why did you decide to come to Japan?"

"Oh, that was because my friend introduced me to Japanese music. I'd always listened to Western rock like hard rock or screamo. And my friend took me to see Dir en Grey (a Japanese metal band) and I really liked them. They reminded me of Western bands, although I didn't understand the lyrics."

She had already dated a Japanese guy before she moved to Japan. She met him during her summer trip.

"He was a cook. I met him at a club in Shibuya. We didn't even speak the same language. I didn't know Japanese that well at the time. But somehow, we hung out. I think he really liked Western girls. We went to Kamakura, and I went to his house sometimes. But I was here just for a month. We dated three weeks, then we talked on Skype.

"It was kind of weird. I'd never liked him that much. He was nice, but he was not so sociable. Maybe it was because I didn't speak Japanese? But then I thought I couldn't be bothered with him. I don't think he thought of me as somebody serious, because I was a foreigner."

"How did it end?"

"He was dating someone else at the same time. I saw pictures of them together. He told me, 'We are just friends.' But then I asked my Japanese friends, 'Is that normal? Hugging her if you are just friends?' They said no. So I messaged her and she said, 'Yeah, he's my boyfriend.'

"She was Filipina. They were together for a long time. They lived together for two years."

Tatsuya

After she broke up with that guy, Michelle met her first serious Japanese boyfriend, Tatsuya.

"I remember everything. I went to a bar in Shinjuku. Tatsuya was sitting there with his American friends who chatted me up. The American guy said, 'Meet my cute Japanese friend!' There were no free seats, so I sat on Tatsuya's lap. We talked about some bands and stuff we liked. He was quite drunk.

"After a while, Tatsuya went somewhere. The American guy said, 'You like Tatsuya, right?' I said, 'Yeah.' He said, 'OK, let's go look for him.' Tatsuya was passed out next to the restroom, leaning against the wall. I got him some water and we kind of slept against the wall together. Everybody passing was saying, 'Oh, you guys are so cute.'

"I think I asked him out. I was quite drunk too. The American guy had said, 'Tatsuya is kind of shy. You should give him your number.' So I asked him, 'Do you want to go out?' And he said, 'Yeah.' We exchanged numbers. Then we went to McDonald's with my Finnish friends and the American guy. In the morning, Tatsuya and I were on the same train. He hugged me. We decided to hang out the next week. After we went home, he texted me saying, 'It was so nice to meet you. See you next week.'

"The next Tuesday, we went out, and we took *purikura*. We were really into each other.

"We started hanging out all the time. Two months later, I had already been to Shizuoka to meet his family. Soon after, he said, 'I have a gift for you,' acting like, *I'm not going to tell you what it is.* It was a key to his house. Everything was quite fast. I moved my stuff into his house and we started living together.

"A couple of months later, in July or August, we went to Bangkok together for my dad's friend's wedding. He met my family. We stayed in a nice apartment with my sisters and their boyfriends. It was pretty fun. We had some fights though. At the wedding, he wouldn't dance. I wanted to dance with him, but he was acting cool. There were some other cute guys, so I just said, 'OK, I'm going to dance with that guy.' Then he got pissed off and we had a fight.

"Otherwise, he never wanted to fight. He never talked about bad things. Actually that was kind of a problem. After I broke up with him, he'd say, 'I know the problem was that we didn't talk.' I said, 'Oh, come on. I tried to talk.'

"I think it's his personality. Maybe something to do with his parents? His relationship with his dad is not so good. Once, I was staying in Shizuoka and his parents were having a huge fight. He tried to calm them down. I heard it from upstairs, so I didn't know what happened. But maybe that's why he doesn't like to fight.

"He wasn't a talkative guy. I didn't like it when we went to a restaurant and he didn't talk. Also, I would have liked him to be more romantic. I'm not that romantic, but he would go to romantic places wearing striped shirts. I hated it, and felt it was kind of disrespectful towards me. He would wear a sweater even when we went to a fancy restaurant.

"It was when I went back to Finland for university that we had a problem. He didn't care to talk on Skype. Not even once in four months. For him, emailing was enough, but I felt that was kind of weird.

"He was a changed person when I got back. He had made new friends because our best friends from the American airbase had left. His new friends were in the American army.

"We were at a house party at the base. Some of his friends hit on me and tried to sleep with me even though Tatsuya was there. I thought, *what the hell?* The American guys were a bad influence on him. He became full of himself.

"Later, he said, 'Because I felt like you hated me.' He was stressed because we were looking for a new house but couldn't find a good one. He was drinking so much and he wouldn't come home or text. Sometimes I left home because I was so pissed off.

"When we finally moved to the new house, his friends said to me, 'You shouldn't trust him. You should check his phone.' I didn't believe them. I was kind of depressed, but I didn't know he was causing it.

"Then I found out that he had been cheating on me. Actually, I had cheated on him once because he was being such an asshole and I was having a shit time with him. I went out with a guy I'd dated before. It was the guy I went to Kamakura with, a long time ago. We went to a wine bar and had a really good time. Sometime later, the Kamakura guy texted me in the morning when I was in Roppongi, and asked me to come to his house. I said 'OK.'

"I told my boyfriend afterwards. I said, 'I want our relationship to be based on trust, so I'm telling you that I cheated.' He said, 'Yeah that's my fault.' And I said, 'Yeah, it is.'

"After that, he became really weird. He was too nice. When I was going to school, he'd say, '*Itterashai* (a greeting you use when a family member leaves your house).'

"A friend of mine knew Tatsuya was sleeping with another girl. So he tried to give me hints. I never believed him, but one night, I checked Tatsuya's phone when he was sleeping just to be sure. Then I saw that he'd been out with that girl the same night. That night, when he had come home, he said he had been to Tower Records. Then he kissed me on the cheek.

"I really wanted to hurt him. I remembered that he'd been thinking that I might be pregnant, even though I wasn't. So I told him I was pregnant with another guy. I said, 'He's good looking and tall. He looks like a model. We will have such a cute baby.' Tatsuya was really pissed off. He started drinking a lot.

"I moved to my friend's house, and went back to Finland later. He lost everything. We'd only lived in our new house for three weeks and I said, 'I'm not paying any money for this new house, because you cheated on me.' He'd quit his

THERE'S SOMETHING I WANT TO TELL YOU

part-time job for the second time that year for some stupid reason. He said, 'I lost all my money, my job, and you.' I said, 'Yeah, that's karma.'"

"What was his job exactly?"

"He only had part-time jobs. In the beginning, he had the same job for a long time. It was just some simple job selling TV channels or making phone sales. He was twenty-two and I was twenty when we met. Then he lost that job. Maybe that's why he started drinking a lot."

"Did he go to university?"

"No. He just finished high school. After that, he came to Tokyo for work."

"But he spoke some English, right?"

"A little bit. But he got better with his English because he had American friends. He was very interested in America. That always annoyed me because I wished he'd been interested in Finland even just a little bit. But he just cared about American bands and stuff.

"He was a good artist, actually. But he didn't draw that much. He just listened to music and bought a lot of records."

Yoshi

"A few months after breaking up with Tatsuya, I went to a bar in Shibuya. It was almost May. My friend told me Tatsuya was coming too. I didn't want to see him. I was out with my friends, drinking on the street in Shibuya before going to the bar. When we decided to go there, I saw someone who was close friends with Tatsuya. He went to check if Tatsuya was there. He checked upstairs, downstairs and said, 'You're safe.'

"That night, I met Yoshi. I talked to Yoshi's best friend first, then I ended up talking to him. It was kind of weird. He was asking me stuff like what food I like. I asked, 'What

73

do you like?' And he said, 'Oh, right now, I like you.' He said cheesy stuff. We took the same train when we went home.

"Shortly after, I went to Hawaii with my sister. I was talking on Facebook with him when I was there. We texted each other saying, 'I miss you.' When I came back, I asked him if he wanted to go to a house party. I think I liked him.

"We hung out together for about a year. It wasn't really like a relationship. We never really said that we were together. Over the first half of the year, I was kind of with him. But after that, we were on and off for about seven months. In the beginning, I thought we were going to be together, but then he would say, 'I'm an artist. I can't concentrate on my art if I have a girlfriend.' But we still hung out all the time. I stayed at his house a couple of nights every week.

"Then we went to the bar in Shibuya again where Yoshi's friend was doing some event that night. Tatsuya was there. I think I told Yoshi. He was fine with that. But I wasn't sure, because I still liked Tatsuya. Yoshi was a really tall, skinny guy who looked like a model and actually did some modeling. But maybe I liked that he liked me? I didn't really have butterflies for him. I might have just felt comfortable with him.

"I remember telling him that I had been hanging out with some other guy because I wasn't sure how he would feel about that. He called me and said, 'That was an April Fools' joke right?' I didn't realize it was April Fools' Day. I said, 'No, it's true.'

"We decided to stop seeing each other. But when we decided that, I was at his house, and spent the night there. In the morning, I took all my stuff and I was about to leave. He said, 'What are you doing?' I said, 'Well, we talked. We are not going to see each other, right?' He said, 'Yeah, I don't know about that anymore.' I said, 'OK, we can hang out, but we're not together.' He said, 'Yeah, that's OK.'

"Then in summer, before I left for the UK, he said he wanted be together seriously. I said, 'Yeah, but what do you mean? You don't even love me.' And he said, 'Maybe I do.' But I didn't like him that way. When I was in the UK, he met a British girl and they started having a long-distance relationship, so I never saw him anymore. We still talk. I don't talk with Tatsuya anymore.

"Yoshi was really a nice guy, unlike my other boyfriends. He would never cheat. He was popular, but he was weirdly insecure. Maybe that's why I didn't like him that much. He cared too much about what people said. He'd say, 'Today, someone said bad stuff about me on the train,' or 'Someone gave me a weird look.'"

Dating in Japan

"Do you think it's hard to date in Japan?"

"It's easy to find dates, but it's hard to find interesting guys. Two weeks before I left Japan, there was one guy I liked who was a little bit younger and had never gone out with a Western girl. We went out on a date, but he was so nervous.

"Also, I went out with another guy, and I thought we had the same interests. But he was too shy and the date was awkward. I'd have to think of what to say all the time. After the date, he sent me a text saying, 'It was so fun,' but I didn't think it was fun at all! I was a bit surprised he said that. Now he asks me out, but I am kind of like, 'Oh no, him again?'"

"Do you think you are popular among Japanese guys?"

"Yeah, I guess so. But I approach them sometimes. Or I just look at them and they'll come to me."

"Have you noticed that you tend to date Asian guys?"

"Yeah. But last year, I went out with a Canadian guy. He was really nice but he wasn't really my type, so it didn't work out. In the UK, I hung out with a Western boy, but he

75

was too shy and quiet. Then I really liked another boy who turned out to be half Japanese. So yeah, I think I do like Asian guys. I don't really like blue-eyed guys, and I also don't really like big eyes. I don't know why."

"But I don't like typical Japanese personalities. They cheat and lie. They think Western women are easy. I feel that some Japanese guys look down on women. I think Western guys are more open and equal. I think they understand me better because we have more in common.

"Last summer, my Japanese friend was heartbroken and drunk and told me I was easy. I was really surprised. I do hang out with guy friends, but that isn't enough reason to say that. I think one of the bartenders told him that. It's kind of Japanese to think that if a girl hangs out with a lot of guys, she's easy. I don't like that."

"How do you know when a Japanese guy likes you?"

"I guess when they text me a lot or they want to meet me. But you usually know."

Discussions

In her stories, Michelle's social life centers on bars and small clubs in Tokyo, where she met most of her boyfriends. The Japanese people who go to these bars and clubs tend to be quite different from most Japanese people. Western-style bars and clubs are relatively rare in Tokyo and the majority of Japanese people don't go there. In addition, the places Michelle frequents tend to be artsy and kind of "alternative".

Tatsuya, for example, doesn't seem to be the average Japanese guy, in the sense that he didn't go to university and has never had a full-time job, something that may or may not be his choice. In a society where work has huge importance, his way of life is considered a bit "alternative."

Yoshi's lifestyle didn't seem mainstream either, since he was an artist.

Michelle seems quite popular in Japan, especially with shy guys. I think part of the reason is how she talks. She's soft-spoken, and that gives the impression that she is kind and caring, which (I think) a lot of Japanese guys find appealing.

6. Frank—Russian women, Japanese women

An American guy dating Japanese women after Russian women

I F YOU WERE TO MEET Frank, you might think he's just your typical white American guy from the Midwest: big, blond, cheerful, and someone who does a lot of positive thinking. But if there's one thing that makes him different, it is that he speaks fluent Russian as his second language.

"Growing up in my state during the Cold War, there were nuclear silos in every direction," Frank said. "They were pointed at Russia. As a child, I thought maybe one day I would see those rockets going out of the prairie and in an hour, everything would be finished. We would be the number one target.

"When I was enrolling in college, I thought I would like to work for NASA. If I could speak Russian, I could be one of the few who do. But my NASA dreams didn't quite come true, because there were a lot of Russians who could speak English, and they were better at math. Still, I thought I really wanted to master Russian. So I went to Moscow for a year and studied Russian at a university. I was twenty-one and for me, it was like being a king. I had dollars and the ruble kept on falling, so I was rich beyond my wildest dreams."

The Brazilian girl

"In college, I got to meet a lot of different new people because I was very active in many organizations. I met a Brazilian girl from Rio de Janeiro. My background is Norwegian, and we're not so touchy-feely. But Brazilians are. I had no defense for holding hands, touching, and kissing all the time. It was very easy to fall in love with her.

"But she came to the university with her boyfriend, and he had been there for quite a long time. In high school, everyone thought those two were going to get married. But we fell in love."

"Did she break up with him?"

"No. Actually he called her father and said, 'Hey I want to marry her,' but he didn't ask her. Her father said yes. And then he told her, 'I talked to your dad and he said yes.' She wasn't too sure if she wanted to do that. But everything was set up to have the wedding in Rio. I thought it was totally shit.

"Even though we never had sex, she was such a good friend and the relationship we had was so good. She was super smart and she was an organic chemist. So I went to buy a ring and proposed to her because if she said yes, I would be happy for the rest of my life.

"This was the purest kind of relationship you can possibly think of. It's a strange thing. But she was sexy and I knew we would be pretty good together. That was my first proposal in life.

"But she married him. And a year later, they got divorced. It didn't work, because he became so obsessive over her. When she got divorced, I was in Russia. But I think I probably would have married her if I had been home.

"Then another summer came and there was summer school for linguists. There was this girl from Montreal. She was forty and I was twenty-three or twenty-four. But she was everything I wanted in a woman. I felt like a better human when I was with her. I decided to fly to Montreal for Thanksgiving after she left. I said, 'I'd like to marry you.' But she said, 'I want to travel. You should think about it more and if you still feel this way in six months, we'll talk about it again. But if you find someone interesting, go for it.' I said, 'Well, actually, I just met this really cute Russian girl at a BBQ.' She was like, 'Why don't you try and see if it works?' I did, and she became my wife. We were married for twelve years."

The Russian wife

"After I had been in Moscow for a year, I was able to speak Russian fairly well. When I came back to my university, I had two more years to finish. I met my wife at a BBQ. They needed a Russian translator for her mother. Her mom was there to see the university. Her mom said, 'Please take care of her.'

"I fell in love with her and we got married. We stayed in married housing on the campus for about a year. She had a J-1 visa, meaning once she finished university, she'd have to go home for two years. But we didn't really want to go to Russia.

"I was lucky, because I met this guy at one of the Japanese culture nights. He was a coordinator in a Japanese sister prefecture of my state. He said, 'I'm really interested in coming back to America, but I need somebody to replace me. Would you be interested in coming to Japan?'

"My wife talked to her mother, and her mother said to her, 'Do you remember as a child that you wanted to learn Japanese? Now would be a very good opportunity to go there.' My home was where my wife was, so I called him back and said OK.

"The Japanese city took care of everything for us. That was the first culture shock because, as Americans, we are very independent and we take care of our own stuff. But the board of education of Japan told us, 'This is your *hanko* (a personal stamp used by Japanese). This is your signature.'

"I was twenty-five and she was twenty. My parents had got married at the same age, so it felt right. Often, one person is more in love than the other, so it was very rare to find people who were both in love the same way.

"She studied English in Japan for a while. She was very intense and serious about studying, but Japanese housewives were not, so it was frustrating for her. The second year, she got a job at a space division in a company. It was very strange, because she studied English and was in a space division, while I studied space technology and taught English.

"We lived in Kanuma (in Tochigi prefecture) but she was commuting to Shin-Yokohama (in Kanagawa prefecture) every day. It was a six-hour round trip! Her Japanese was amazing by that time. She passed level 1 (the most difficult level of the Japanese Language Proficiency Test). You could say she was focused, but it was almost too much.

"Three years ago, my wife had been traveling quite a bit. She said, 'OK, I need to go to a conference in Europe.' But it was actually a job interview. One day, she told me that she'd found a job in Europe. She said, 'I would like to be there for half a year by myself.' That was the first step towards separating. We ended up getting a divorce a year later.

81

"I didn't want a divorce. I'd always felt that divorces make things so sour. You have to make it a nice ending. I think you have a lot of choice in life as to how to approach things. So I chose not to fight it and not to demonize her. I told my family, 'Don't speak ill of her. We were the only people who could fix it. Nobody else has lived my life and spent twelve years with this woman.'

"Almost every girlfriend I'd ever had, it never ended in a fight. We just separated as good friends. Even the end of my marriage was like that. We went to Town Hall and signed it away. It was sad and it hurt like hell. But 'if you love a bird, set it free. If it comes back, the bird is yours.' Well, it didn't.

"It was a rough year going into divorce. I read a lot of self-help books."

"Did it help?"

"You betcha! I searched for a book called *Five Languages of Love*. That one talks about how each person expresses love in the way they want to receive it. There are people who have learned—maybe through their parents—that love is giving gifts. I'd always given gifts, thinking I was showing my love. But I'd never said 'I love you' or 'I really appreciate you.' For some people, if they're not hugged, they won't feel loved. I thought that was exactly what happened."

"So what do you think her language of love was?"

"I think it was acts of love, meaning washing dishes or cleaning the house. Another thing I learned though books was that women have very different mind wiring. If men have a stressful day, we can just put it away—put it in a box and pick it up tomorrow. But women have to unwind. And that means to talk about it. I am always trying to fix. But the book says she doesn't really want to fix it. All she wants you to do is listen. That would've been nice to know earlier on."

The Cosmo girl

"For me, Russian women are kind of like a narcotic. They are very bad for you, but they are so good for you too. They are so volatile. They like to be treated like princesses plus, plus. You must always pay for them. They'll never go on a second date if you don't pay. And you have to know all the different flowers. You have to know never to get yellow flowers, or an even number of flowers. You can have a beautiful bouquet of roses, but if it's a dozen, she'll treat you like shit. So if you get a dozen, just throw one away, or buy a lot of flowers so she can't count.

"With my Russian girlfriend I met in Japan, it was fabulous. Best sex ever. It was because of her praise. I think maybe the first or second time she came over, she said, 'I had no idea how good it could be.' That set the bar very high, but it made me want to be a better lover. I had a Russian friend who said, 'She was faking it. Five times is impossible.' I said, 'I don't care actually. After the first two or three times, why would she fake it?' Men are driven. It's competition. Wow, five! Let's go for seven!

"She reinforced it. She'd say, 'When you finger me, can you be behind me?' or, 'Could you nibble my ear?' I thought, *thank you so much for telling me this! I'll do it all the time!* She also gave me the best blowjob of my entire life. I asked, 'How the hell did you learn this?' She said, '*Cosmopolitan.*' I thought, *I want to find that article, because I want to copy it and take it along with me whenever I'm in a relationship.*

"But then she started having some personal problems. She started pushing me away because she didn't want me to be a part of it."

The Japanese girl

"There was a meetup party. I saw this really cute girl and I said, 'Hi.' I was sitting by her. Apparently we were sitting so close that we looked good together. Three times that night, people asked if she was my wife.

"Japanese women are very accommodating. Not a lot of self. 'Oh, you want to go there? Let's go there. You want to watch this movie? Let's go!' For the most part, you are allowed a lot of freedom. That's nice, but on the other hand, it doesn't feel as equal. I think in the long run, it's hard because you want someone a little bit more dynamic.

"My current girlfriend is changing a little bit because she knows I want her to. But in the beginning, it was frustrating. When I said, 'Hey, where would you like to go for dinner?' She said, 'Oh, anywhere is OK.' That was nice, but sooner or later you'll think, 'You know, I'd like you to actually have an opinion.' I read a book that said, 'Every man wants to be a knight in shining armor.' Women need to give you an opportunity to be that knight in shining armor. It requires some sort of request.

"Right now she's searching for a new job, so I help her with that. But there's something I'd like to discuss more. We Americans are always meddling and thinking about everyone else's business. I think a lot of Japanese in general aren't very interested in world affairs. Putin invaded Ukraine. Damn sure, if you had a Russian wife, you would have talked about this. Japanese wife, probably never. The Japanese will listen to you but that's it. Very little participation. But I'd love to hear what Japanese people think.

"There are Japanese women who have studied abroad or traveled a lot. They have opinions. They are totally different type of women. But, there are others who just want to get a husband so they can be housewives.

"She was a home-stay student in Minnesota for a few months. Her English is very good. She says, 'I don't speak very well." But very rarely do I say something that she doesn't understand.

"I think she's one of those people who doesn't want to be the same as everybody else. She pushed herself in other directions that were totally different from everything that's Japanese. She doesn't like sushi. She loves bread all the time."

"Do you think she is interested in the US rather than foreign countries, in general?"

"I think, yeah. But if I said 'Hey, let's go to Paris' she would love to travel, and that's a big thing for me because when I was married, we traveled almost every year. One Christmas we went to Russia, and next Christmas we went to the States. And then we had one free Christmas to go somewhere we actually wanted to go. Hawaii, Thailand, Cambodia, Coastal Australia, New Zealand…

"My relationship is getting to the point where my next test is to see how strong this relationship is. Maybe this summer I'll take her back to the US. Going on a trip is a really good way to see the true person. And I think she should see my family so she sees what she's getting into. I have some crazy family."

"How long have you guys been together?"

"Since after the earthquake, so almost three years. People ask me, 'What's going to happen?' For me, I want to kind of take it slow. She's twenty-seven. I'm forty-two. I don't feel like I need to rush into another marriage. I'm glad she doesn't pressure me. My boss was with his girlfriend for twelve years before getting married. My feeling is that if you stay together for a long time in a good relationship, it's a good indicator of how long you can be together after marriage."

"How's your sex life?"

"The Russian girl made me want to try harder. It was such a compliment to me. Honestly, when guys have sex, that's what they want. Another thing with her is that it was so electrifying. In an average morning and night, I could get her maybe four or five times. Like I said, it got to be almost like a competition. She said, 'When we get older, I don't know if I could keep up.' I think I will slow down! But that chemistry was so fabulous.

"I had some good experiences with Japanese women and some not so great ones. So, this one, I'd say she isn't so active in the whole process. From my perspective, I want creativity. When I was in Russia and had many Russian girlfriends, I learned some of the things I liked and didn't like.

"I think Japanese women have seen so much porn, they think they need to say things that—if you translate them— don't sound so sexy. I think in some porn, there's something like 'it hurts.' I don't see anything sexy about this at all! Why do you say this? If it does, I'll stop! I also think that when speaking in a foreign language, there's sometimes a disconnect. You can be bolder and say things you would never say in your native language."

Japanese women tend to say "No! No!" in bed, while Western women tend to say "Yes! Yes!"

"What does she do?"

"She is working as a receptionist. But she wants to find a salaried job, a real job, which I agree with. Then if she wants to take a week off, she'll still get paid. That'll give us a chance to do more things together."

"Has she always had part-time jobs?"

"Yeah. I don't think she's really had a full-time job."

"Did she go to university? What did she study?"

"She... I'll have to check on that. That's a really good question. I never really got into asking about her studies. Or she wasn't maybe too happy with the college. Overall, I think she wants to be a good salesperson. She studies a lot about how to give presentations, or how to have etiquette. These things are important for her."

"Have you noticed any cultural differences?"

"Culture-wise or character-wise, she is always thinking of other people very much, to her own detriment sometimes.

For example, an old man is walking in front of us. Sometimes, she'll say to me, 'Hey, get out of the way.' Wait a minute! I'm not the bad one here. I have the right to be on this street too. She doesn't have to choose for me. I choose for myself. Americans have a very strong sense of 'I.' I feel all of us have equal responsibility to be good to each other. But the grandpa has just as much responsibility to step out of my way.

"One amazing thing about her is that she never asks me questions about what I did on weekends or who is in the pictures. I love it! Other girls ask these dangerous, leading questions. 'Who is this person in the picture?' I have to frame my answer really fast because they're asking this for some damn good reason. She doesn't do that. It's nice, because it means she trusts me."

Discussions

During the interview, there was a Sri Lankan woman sitting next to us. She was listening to our conversation and eventually she started speaking Russian to Frank. (It turned out that her late husband was Russian.) She admired Frank. Before she left, she said, "What he is saying is more than two hundred percent right! He is so positive about everything." Frank is a really nice guy. He was always helpful, and all the people I met through him turned out to be very nice too.

As nice as Frank is, his communication style is very fast-paced, and I think a lot of Japanese people may find it difficult to keep up with it. I would imagine that his Japanese girlfriend's communication style is quite different from Frank's. This won't necessarily be a big problem since his current girlfriend doesn't seem to be very expressive or opinionated; she is accommodating. Frank talked very little about her compared to his other girlfriends. It might be because she doesn't talk about herself a lot.

7. Sabina—My husband knows my body

How a Russian model got into a successful marriage

$\int$ ABINA GAVE ME A DIFFERENT impression from what I had imagined as a "Russian model." When I arrived at Ikebukuro to meet her, she was already there; she was early. She wasn't as tall as I had expected and she was wearing very simple clothes. She was friendly and down to earth.

────◄ ♥ ►────

"I was on the train with my mom on the way to another city for a summer holiday," she said. "There was a beautiful girl in the same compartment. I was fourteen and she was seventeen. My mom started to talk to her. The girl said she was a model and she told us her story.

"I thought, *wow, she's beautiful. I'd like to be the same!* Her pictures were really beautiful. My mom said, 'When you go back, you can go to modeling school.' So I went to the modeling school for three months. It was so hard for me, because I needed to wear pin heels and high heels. My usual style was boyish.

"The school had two levels. I finished one. The next level was for girls who would actually become models. But they didn't invite me. I wasn't upset. I thought I needed to be stronger. I went to another school. A manager looked at me and said, 'Yeah, you can work.' So I started to work. I went to Moscow for fashion shows and started doing magazine jobs. It was really nice.

"In Russia, the modeling market was really small. And it wasn't as 'clean' as it is in Japan. When it comes to casting in Japan, they check my face and my portfolio and if I'm their type, they'll hire me. But in Russia, they asked me if I had a sponsor. I said, 'Excuse me?' I didn't need a sponsor. Why would I?

"A sponsor is some rich man who can pay for me. He doesn't need to be in the industry. He just needs to be rich. For example, if you are a designer and need a model, a sponsor will come to you and say, 'Can you use my model? I'll give you money.'

"Once I said, 'I won't sleep with this man. I won't take the job.' It seemed like a dirty kind of business. I didn't want to sell my body. My body was really important to me. I didn't want to share. I went to Moscow and a lot of people said, 'Can you change into a swimsuit?' It felt weird to me. So I went back to my city and said, 'I don't like it.'"

At 17, she got an opportunity to work in Japan. From that time, she started traveling back and forth between Japan (to work) and Russia (to study).

"When they asked me if I wanted to go to Japan, my manager said, 'Come on, she cannot work as a model in Japan.' She didn't believe in me. But then I came to Japan and worked. After three or four years, I took my magazine and some pictures from my job and gave them to her. She was so shocked."

The bad guy

When Sabina was nineteen, she dated her first Japanese guy.

"I met him in a club. I was out with my friends. It was a big club in Roppongi, but they're closed now. He just came up to me and we started to talk. He was handsome and looked cool. His style was good."

"Did he talk to you in Japanese?"

"No, English. Well, English and Japanese. We talked a little bit and he asked for my number. We met a couple of times and he invited me to dinner. At that time, I had to go back to Russia, so I went back. Then after two months, he said, 'Let's live together. Please come to visit me in Japan.' So I came to visit him and we started living together. But it didn't work out.

"It was because of the language barrier, and because I was too young for him. He wanted to get married. Or he had to. He was thirty-three at the time and he said he needed to get married before thirty-five. I would not get married to somebody who had to get married.

"And he kept some secrets from me. He hadn't told me he had a kid. One day, he said, 'Would you like to go to Okinawa with me?' I said, 'Yeah, let's go.' Then he said, 'I cannot find a ticket for you.' I said, 'That's kind of strange.' He said, 'I need to go because of my work.' Then he went to Okinawa. And after that he said, 'It was really nice. I met my kid.' I said, 'Sorry, what?' He said, 'I dated a girl and she said she was pregnant, but I said I wasn't ready to have a family and kids. So we broke up.' I thought, *how can you do that shit to a woman?*

"Of course, I started to wonder whether I could stay with this man. I thought about his job and about everything he had done. I thought, 'No, he's not the man I want to spend my life with.' He showed off to people that he had money, which he had. When we went out, he would buy Dom Pérignon."

"What was his job?"

"I still don't know, because he didn't share it with me. I knew he had a karaoke bar. He opened it when we were dating. I think he said when he was young, he was a host in a host club (a place where women pay to interact with attractive men; the best hosts are said to earn more than $10,000 a month). So maybe that's how he made money."

"He didn't give me a chance to work. He would say, 'You don't need to work.' But how could I call my parents? I needed money. Back then we didn't have Skype. So he said, 'I need to give you money,' and just gave me 10,000 yen (about $100) a week.

"He opened his karaoke bar. One day, I was with my friend and I was drunk. I went to see him. When I went inside, he said, 'Hey, you cannot visit me here.' But he didn't tell me the reason. I left and I was so mad at him. It was Halloween. I wanted to enjoy spending time with him.

"Next morning, he said, 'You need to go back to Russia. I don't want to stay with you anymore.' I said, 'OK, I'll leave.' Maybe he thought I would say 'I don't want to go.' But I left.

"I had a friend who had lived in Japan for a long time and spoke good Japanese. She came to his house once and said, 'This guy sucks. He's not a good person.' Now I know it. Two days after we broke up, she called me and said, 'How's everything?' I said, 'He says he wants to break up with me.' She said, 'Can I talk to him?' She talked him for so long in Japanese. She said to me, 'It's better for you to leave him.' These last two days, he was hugging and holding me saying, 'I'm sorry. I'm a bad guy.' But I left anyway.

"I called my friend and asked her if she had an apartment. She did and she let me stay. She said, 'You can stay with me just for a bit before you find a job.' I talked to my agency and went back to work.

"After one or two years, I talked to him again on the phone. I asked him, 'Is everything OK?' He said, 'The girl I had the kid with came to see me and we had sex. And she's pregnant again.' I didn't understand this."

The good guy

Sabina only dated the host guy for a couple of months. Fortunately, she also met a good guy.

"I met him about the same time I was dating the host guy. It was also in a club in Roppongi but a different one. We just talked. He was so calm and quiet. When I met him, there were some signs that he would be my man. I thought he was a really nice guy and he had a beautiful smile. But I thought it wouldn't be so nice to call him at the time, because the host guy would be jealous. But in my heart, I wanted to call him.

"I was waiting for the perfect time. When I broke up with the host guy, I called him. He started helping me use the subway because I didn't know how. He bought me a Suica. I still have it."

She took the Suica out of her purse. Suica is a rechargeable electronic ticket you can use in the Tokyo area. Hers was battered and what was written on the surface was barely legible. She kept it for more than nine years. It was one of her first memories of him.

"He showed me Tokyo and took to me to Meiji Shrine. It was really beautiful. My ex-boyfriend hadn't shown me Japan at all. Instead, we just spent time at home. It was very nice to see different parts of Japan.

"I started spending time with him as a friend. After two months, we were meeting almost every day. And then, I started to become jealous. He was my man, and I didn't want to share. My heart said, 'I want to be with this man.'"

"Did you tell him?"

"No! But I think he could understand. He was sixteen years older than me. At the time he was thirty-four or thirty-five."

"Did he have a lot of experience dating?"

"No. He had dated one Japanese girl for thirteen years, but they had broken up. They had started dating in high school. He asked her to marry him, but she wasn't ready. She was busy with her job. Then when she asked him to marry her, he said, 'No it's not the time. Just wait a little bit.' And then they broke up.

"We started to spend even more time together. My roommate said, 'I need to move to a smaller apartment.' So I needed to find a room, but I couldn't rent an apartment. My agency had an apartment, but it was twice as expensive. So I talked to him. He said, 'Move here and stay with me.' It would be my first experience living with somebody seriously.

"Before I moved, we checked some other apartments. He said, 'We need to pay half and half. Are you ready to pay for the apartment?' I thought about it and said, 'You know, I don't spend so much time at home. Maybe there's no point. Your apartment would be enough for us.' His apartment was really small from a Russian point of view. But I didn't really care, because it was for living with somebody I loved.

"So I took my suitcase and a small lamp and moved in. He said, 'Throw it away.' I said, 'It's mine. I bought it.' Actually I didn't buy it. I found it in the garbage. For me, finding something in garbage was like 'Wow.' In Russia, that doesn't happen. I moved to his house with the lamp and a toy giraffe he had bought for me in Yokohama. When I said,

'Wow, I really love this giraffe!' he bought it for me. It's still with us in our apartment.

"He's so calm and gentle. I liked everything about him from the beginning. For me, it was a big point how he ate. I liked how he held his fork and knife. You know how Japanese people eat ramen? When he ate ramen in front of me, he didn't make noises. Now he does, but in the beginning, no.

"He wanted to introduce Japanese food to me. My ex-boyfriend would eat *natto* and just say, 'I'm sure you don't like it.' But my husband would say, 'It doesn't smell good, but it's very good for you. Try!' If he puts it that way, that makes me want to try. He taught me a lot about life and culture in Japan."

She still had to go back to Russia to go to university.

"I went back to Russia. He said, 'Let's go somewhere and spend time together.' I said, 'Well, first, you come to Russia. You should see my country. You should see my family.' He came to Russia. It was my sister's wedding. It was his first time visiting Russia, and he met about a hundred people at the wedding. The party lasted all day. He was Japanese, so everyone looked at him, saying, 'Let's get drunk! Let's drink vodka!' My grandma asked me, 'Who is this man?' I said, 'He's my future husband.'

"We spent time in Russia and I showed him around. Then he left because he needed to work. I went back to study. I stayed in Russia for six months. We chatted on Skype every day."

Then they went on a trip to Thailand.

"On Saint Valentine's Day, we went to Pattaya. He asked me if I wanted to go out to dinner. I said, 'No, I just want to spend time with you in the hotel.' So we were sitting on our bed. You know, he made a heart with roses. He said, 'I want to say something to you,' and he said, 'Would you like to be my wife?' in Russian! I said, 'Yes!' He said, 'Really?'

"It happened so fast. He said, 'I don't have a ring now, because I want to buy one with you. So tomorrow, we'll go and buy a ring.'

"The next day, we went to a mall and looked for a ring and we found one. I said, 'Now you need to propose to me again.' He said, 'No, I did it already!'

"When I went back to Russia to study, he said, 'You have to come to Japan.' He prepared for the wedding ceremony. We had a ceremony at Meiji Shrine. Then I went back to Russia to prepare for a ceremony in Russia. After three months, he came to Russia for the ceremony. We did it in a church. Usually in Russia, when people get married in a church, they can't divorce. If you do it just on paper, you can. But not if you do it in a church. So my mom's friend said, 'It's a really big step. It means he's ready to stay forever.'

"We went back to Japan together. And my agency gave me a contract and I started to work with them. So I was stuck here.

"I'd never in my life imagined that somebody would be crazy enough to propose to me. I didn't think somebody would be so extreme as to marry a Russian. Marry a crazy girl like me."

"How are you crazy?"

"I would say I'm not such a good a wife. I know some women who are amazing wives and I think their husbands are so lucky. But I think marriage is a job for two. It needs to be half and half. If you don't do that, you cannot stay together.

"I remember when he proposed, he said, 'I'm ready to be stuck with a Russian in my life.' I said, 'I say this to you, but I will not stay at home cooking for you. I won't do all this house cleaning so that you come home and just relax. It's going to be fifty-fifty. When you work and I don't, I'll do something, but when you are not working, you'll need to help me on Saturday and Sunday.' He said, 'I'm OK with that.'"

"So, does he do housework?"

"Now, no! In the beginning, yes. But he's working hard and I'm thankful to him. He's paying for our house and our meals. But sometimes, I say, 'Let's clean together.' He says, 'It's going to be the New Year. We need to clean everything.' Once a year he is stuck in the bath for three hours. I cannot do that."

In Western countries, this might be called "spring cleaning," but it's more common in Japan to do it before the New Year.

"But I'm Russian. So I say to him, 'Don't make a mistake. Don't tell me how things are supposed to be in Japan. We need to make our family.' For me it's very important to say 'we.' It shouldn't be 'my husband,' or 'I.' It should be 'we do.'"

"Sometimes, I do things that seem strange to Japanese people. For example, on the train, if I see young people sitting and old people standing, I say, 'Move your ass.' My husband and I fight sometimes about this. I say, 'You know, in Russia…' but he says, 'Yeah, but this is Japan.' I don't care. This type of stuff is hard for us."

"What do you guys like to do?"

"I love to go out, go to a park, and make friends. Sometimes I want to stay at home if I'm tired of people. But usually I'm out. He's not a big fan of making a lot of friends. He's nice with people, but he doesn't make friends."

"Do you think you take more initiatives in your relationship?"

"I think so. He's happy to do something I ask him to do. Sometimes I get tired of this. I say, 'Tell me something you want to do.' But he says, 'No, I'm happy to go with what you want to do. I just want to spend time with you.' It's really nice of him, but I don't think he's one hundred percent happy.

"For example, I cannot see movies where people kill each other. I want to watch something romantic. But I understand he's a man. He wants to see action films. One time, I said, 'OK, I can go with you.' And when it was over, I was tired and had a huge headache. The movie was 3D and my seat was shaking. He said, 'No, we take a break and watch another one.' I said, 'What?' He said, "Yeah, let's see another one!' And I saw his face and he was so excited. I didn't have a choice! So we watched another one and I fell asleep in the middle. Maybe I'm bad this way. I need to be nicer. He always watches musicals or romantic comedies with me.

"Actually, we fought a lot from the beginning, when we started living together. After a year, we started to fight about stupid things, like about the house. When I was younger, I would break things like lamps. If I had spoken enough Japanese, maybe it wouldn't have happened. I was mad, not only at him, but at myself for not being able to explain. Then I'd wonder, *why do I break these glasses? They didn't do anything to me.* Now we can just talk. But he's stubborn and I'm stubborn.

"If he gets angry, he might say something, but usually he doesn't. It's a little bit hard for me, because if I ask, 'What do you want for dinner?' he will say, 'Whatever you can cook.' I'm like, 'Just say something!' I have a friend in the same situation. Japanese guys don't want to make trouble. It's easy for them, but not easy for me."

"What do you think of Japanese guys in bed?"

"You know, for me, that's the best thing. With my man, everything has been good from the beginning. I cannot say about Japanese guys in general, because I haven't had a lot in my life, but my husband is best for my body and for my feelings. It's maybe why our marriage stays alive. He knows my body.

"Sometimes I'd say, 'Let's do it in a car.' In Japan, it's not possible. They take a shower and clean their bodies because they want to relax. In Russia, some people do it everywhere. Sometimes in the kitchen. It's sexy. I say, 'Oh, nice car!' But he says, 'Come on, no!' Now I think it's weird that people do it in a car."

"Has he lived abroad before?"

"No, but he went to San Francisco and San Diego for three months on a road trip. So he's kind of international. He's not a typical Japanese guy. After living in Japan for eleven years, I cannot imagine staying with a typical Japanese guy. If something happens with our marriage, he'll be the last man in my life."

"How's he not typical?"

"On the train, he lets ladies have a seat first. Typical Japanese guys wouldn't do that. He always carries heavy bags. He opens the door. He doesn't take food from my plate even though I finished. He always asks first."

"Where did he learn those things?"

"I think from American movies. When we started dating and I was in Russia, he sent me a letter. It was in Russian. He had asked somebody to translate. He wrote, 'I'm sorry, I cannot be American style and say "I love you" and hug you always, but I'll try to learn.' He really likes Cameron Diaz. He must have seen romance movies and learned from them. I don't see that he learned it from his family or people around him.

"When we started dating, I held his hand, but he was shy in the beginning. I said, 'Hey, you are my man. If I want to touch your ass, I will touch your ass.' But sometimes he gets shy. When we are on the train, I say 'Kiss me.' Actually, I don't really want to kiss him right then, but I'm kind of testing him to see if he has changed over the years.

"In the beginning, we always wanted to spend time together and it was so sweet. Then after two or three years, I was busy with my job and he was busy too. We lost something in our love. Sometimes, I miss the time when we were just friends. Back then, if I said, 'Oh, I want a giraffe,' he would say, 'OK, I'll buy it!' It was easy. But now it's more like, 'OK, we don't have to work today. Let's stay at home and just take care of our house.' It's changed."

Discussions

I can't help but think that Sabina's husband seems like a really good guy. I also admire Sabina for her determination to become a model and find her way to Japan. In addition to that, she seems to have a knack for finding the right guy. Even though she dated the wrong guy first, she made a good decision to leave him and got together with the right guy.

In their relationship, Sabina is usually the one who takes initiatives. Her husband goes along with whatever she likes to do. This is not a bad thing, because I get the impression that her husband is genuinely happy being this way.

I have similar experiences with one of my Japanese colleagues. When we go to lunch together, we usually go for whatever I want to eat because I tend to know what I want. When we buy something for the office, he goes with whatever I like. He has a Japanese wife and it's the same: his wife is the one who takes initiatives. But when he has something important to say about work, he expresses his thoughts one way or another, because it's something he truly cares about.

I think Sabina's husband is similar. It's just how he is. And when he does care about something, he expresses it, just like he did when they went to see action films.

8. James—Sleeping with 100 Japanese girls

From a virgin to Charisma Man

"THIS BRITISH GUY, JAMES, HE'S dated more than a hundred Japanese girls," said a friend of mine. James was a highly successful man. He manages a multi-national company.

On the day of the interview, James took me to a small bar on a narrow street. There was a small table with chairs outside. "I thought you wanted a quiet place, so I booked this table," he said. Then he added, "But I only have time until nine pm. Is that OK?"

As soon as we sat down at the table, he took out his laptop and started checking his email. "He is a busy businessman, after all," I thought.

"I was brought up by my mother in England till I was twenty-one," he said. "We moved house fifteen times because of my mother's work and her bad taste in men. She got divorced three times. I was brought up in the countryside. When I was home, I'd usually just take my gun and my fishing stuff and go to the mountains to hunt for food.

"Then I spent two years backpacking through Iran, Afghanistan, Pakistan, and India. And then I spent eighteen or nineteen years in Japan. First, I was selling stuff on the street. Then I worked in a Japanese company for two years to learn Japanese. When I was twenty-five, I set up my first company and I've run three multi-national companies since then."

"Didn't your mother's romantic life bother you?"

"It did, and that's why I hadn't had a date till I was twenty-two. I was interested in girls, but I didn't want that kind of hassle. I was really shy and introverted. I was a virgin until twenty-two. I was in a boarding school, so it was only men. But then from twenty-one to twenty-three, I was in jungles and in the Himalayas and if there were people, they were religious people, so there was no dating. You would get killed if you spoke to a woman you're not related to.

"I met a Japanese girl in Pakistan where I was studying Islam in a mosque for a month. Then I lived outside the Himalayas for a couple of months. I had always met refugees from Afghanistan, so I started going to Afghanistan and volunteered to run a refugee camp during the war there. Then the Taliban came and I had to leave. So I was back in Pakistan and I met her. There was a guy passing on the street and he grabbed her. She was being attacked. I fought with him and saved her.

"I was living in a very religious village, and I invited her there. But women and men lived separately there. Then I told her I was going to meet the Dalai Lama. I spent a few months teaching the refugees and the monks there. She stayed there helping children in an orphanage. We started going out, and we were together for about two years.

"She came down south with me and then while I was there, she came back to Japan. Later, I came to Japan by chance. I had no plan to come here. I only came because in Thailand, the place I stayed caught fire and burnt down. I lost all my clothes and all I had to wear was a tablecloth. I had $400 left, so I thought of going to Japan just for three months, making one million yen (about $10,000) and traveling again.

"How did you make the money?"

"Well, it's easy. I only worked for two or three hours a day for a week. I sold stuff I bought in Pakistan, India, Thailand, and Tibet. Things like handicrafts.

"My plan was to save that money and buy horses in Mongolia. But I was interested in Japan, so I thought I would spend two years here and study the Japanese language and business. I bought a suit, paid some rent, and went for a Japanese company—a trading company. The salary was very low, but I did it just out of interest. I only got 140,000 yen (about $1,400) a month and I worked from nine am to ten pm.

"But I didn't like the hierarchy and unpaid overtime. So I borrowed a million dollars from an English company and created my own company. I created factories in China, Malaysia, and Taiwan so I could travel there for work."

"Where did you get your entrepreneurial spirit from?"

"I always had it. When I was eleven or twelve, I wanted to see my father who lived in Canada, but my mother didn't have much money so I dug in the garbage. My village was a couple of thousand years old and I walked through the fields and looked for broken glass. I dug up bottles that were a couple of hundred years old and sold them to pay for my airplane ticket."

"How did your first relationship end?"

"That girl became like a sister instead of a girlfriend. And I'd never had a girlfriend before, so I didn't know what kind of girlfriend she'd be. I'd never even held hands with a girl. We are still in touch.

"The second girl I dated in Japan was the best friend of my first girlfriend. She was a news announcer on TV and a director. She was really kind, but she lived far away in another prefecture so I couldn't meet her a lot. It didn't work out.

"Then I decided not to open up again because my first girl had cheated on me and so had my second girl. I started playing around a lot. I decided to only have sex, but never trust girls. I went to bars and brought back girls to my house. Usually Shinjuku or Yokohama. I started going to Roppongi as well.

"At first, I wasn't used to picking up girls, but if you go to foreigner bars, girls approach you too. I didn't have to say anything. If it was Shinjuku or Roppongi, I could always get laid if I wanted to."

What he calls "foreigner bars" are western-style bars— the kind of bars you usually see in America or Europe. Most Japanese people prefer Japanese-style bars where seats are assigned, as in a restaurant. They are happy to stick with their own group. Semi-private seats are popular because then, they don't have to see other customers.

As a consequence, Japanese people who go to Western-style bars are often the ones who like Western culture. A lot of the girls who go there regularly are into Western guys.

"Normally, they weren't necessarily easy girls, but some of them just wanted to have sex with foreigners. A lot of them would also actually date foreigners. When I came here around 1996, some girls didn't want to meet a foreigner at the station, because they didn't want to be seen with a foreigner. Also, some parents would not let their daughters date foreigners, so they slept with foreigners until they were twenty-seven and then, suddenly, broke up with them and married a Japanese guy the next day. But then, after two years, they would start to sleep with foreigners again while still staying married.

"You see, a lot of girls who are dating foreigners pretend to be single, but they are actually married or have Japanese boyfriends separately. Some girls idolize foreigners because of American films and such. They think all foreign guys are cool and handsome. But the girls are not very interesting themselves. Foreign guys also tend to think of themselves as cool even though they don't really have good qualities."

The Irish pub girl

"It was ten years ago. I met a girl in an Irish pub in Shinjuku. She was studying to be a Japanese teacher, and working part time at the pub. I dated her. Then I found out she was cheating on me, so I broke up with her. I should've known better because I met her in a bar.

"Six months later, I met her twice by chance, once in the street and the next day in a bar. I still really liked her. She was crying and saying, 'I'll never do that again.' So I dated her again. And then, suddenly, she broke up with me. I'd thought we were doing fine. She said, 'It hurts me because you don't trust me.' I said, 'No, I trust you.' But she said, 'No, you don't.' I couldn't understand why she was saying that.

"A year later, I ran into her in Shibuya. She was with another foreigner and said, 'So, this is my husband.' I said, 'Congratulations. When were you married?' She said, 'One year ago.' Then I realized it:

"The second time I dated her, I was the one she was cheating with.

"Last year I ran into her again by chance. I met her twice in the same night. The first time, in a bar in Shibuya, and then in another standing bar. She was giving her number to another foreigner. She was still married.

"A lot of girls were like that. So many other girls I dated said, "You are the first foreigner I've ever met." Then the phone would ring and they were like, 'Hi, I'll call back later.' I said, 'Hey, you're speaking English.' They said, 'That's a Japanese friend. We always speak English together.' It was clearly a lie. This happened so many times. I can't even count.

"There's this one girl I know. She's my friend's friend and she wants to have sex all the time. We were drinking together and she was like, "I'm just going to go out. I'm going to Shibuya station." She went to Shibuya station, got a guy to pick her up, screwed him in a hotel, and came back. She was really hot, but when I met her, she was constantly phoning. She was trying to find a guy to sleep with. She went through fifteen numbers and one guy called. She was like, 'OK, just in a car is fine. Give me a minute.'

"Some girls are like that. Some are lonely, and some want to get out of their parents' house. Others idolize white guys and want to have a mixed-race baby, or they want to live abroad. When I first came to Japan, a lot of girls wanted to practice their English for free."

Roppongi society

"In Roppongi, you see groups of girls in their thirties. Some of them are pretty, but a lot of them are not. They are full of themselves. Everyone thinks that a girl in Roppongi will have sex with anyone. Guys will talk to her because they want to have sex the same night. But she thinks she's popular, even though she's not pretty. She doesn't understand why. Just like a lot of girls who go to Vancouver and think they are popular.

But it's actually because Japanese girls have a reputation for being easy.

"Roppongi's bars are divided by social classes. Now, at certain bars in Roppongi Hills, there are rich guys. Japanese girls try hard to dress up to impress them, even though they can barely afford it. Some cheap clubs are for US military. The girls are in their teens and they want to have sex with GIs. Some bars have black guys, so some girls are there to find them. There are also bars where English teachers hang out. So it's like a class system. If you go to a classy bar and say you are an English teacher, girls will leave. If I go to a black club, no girl will be interested in me.

"If you are rich, you can sleep with a girl any time. That's why I always tell them I'm a salesman instead of an executive. I don't want to attract gold diggers. If it's a rich guys' bar, they will lose interest immediately. If it's an ordinary bar, they'll be interested. They will ask what I do. But it's completely different when I tell them I'm an executive.

"When I first came here, not many foreigners spoke Japanese. But I did, so it was easy to meet girls. I never really had a strategy. I was just honest and interested in meeting people. If I am obvious, girls can tell. So I just get to know girls first, and sometimes it can get to be more than just friendship.

"In my mid-twenties to mid-thirties, I dated a couple of girls seriously, but mostly I was just messing around."

"Were most girls looking specifically for foreign guys?"

"Not all, but most of them were. Even the ones who usually dated Japanese guys had a little bit of interest. Like, they wanted to try at least once."

How he picks up Japanese girls

"Where did you meet all these girls?"

"Everywhere. When I was a salesman I used to meet girls on the train. I got at least two or three numbers every day."

"How did you talk to them?"

"What is the next station? What time does the train leave? If she's got earphones and takes them off and puts them on again, she doesn't want to talk. But if she's not putting them on again, I know she's curious. Then she will say something like, 'Oh, you speak Japanese? Are you working?' Well, I also got approached by girls quite actively, so it depends.

"It's just like business. You can't make luck, but you can make opportunities for luck. Actually, that's the example I give at business seminars sometimes. Some people say I was lucky that I founded my first company out of the garbage. I became CEO of one of the best companies in Britain because of a guy who sat next to me on a plane. He offered me a job, and I said no. A year later, I met him in Yokohama, a week after I quit my job, and he hired me that day. You make your luck, because you decide if you're going to talk to someone. And you decide how you talk to them. I didn't try to sell anything. I tried to treat people like human beings.

"If I am trying to get on the train and there're a lot of queues, why not stand behind a cute girl and ask for directions? If there's no cute girl at all, I sit next to an empty seat and double the chance that a cute girl will sit next to me. If I see a cute girl walking down the corridor, I look at her for a second so she sees me, and then I look away so she doesn't feel embarrassed, and she then sits next to me. I can't make her sit next to me or want to talk to me, but I can increase the chance. It's the same in business.

"I have friends who are just complete players. They walk down the street and ask every girl out. They get way more numbers than I do. I'm embarrassed because they have no shame. One day, we walked down the street in Roppongi, and got three or four phone numbers in just ten minutes.

"A bar in Shibuya used to be a good place to meet girls, but now it's not, because the same group of Turkish guys hit on girls sitting at every table. The girls are not interested, but the guys just keep going and going until the girls leave. And they go to the next table and do the same thing again. Girls stopped coming. Now there are almost no cute girls there, because the Turkish guys have been going out for almost two years and irritating the girls. They get laid sometimes, but the girls won't come back."

The NGO girl

"I've had six or seven real girlfriends in Japan. After I had played around for a while, I was in First Kitchen (a fast-food restaurant) in Shinjuku. A girl next to me spilt a drink and I cleaned it up. She had a lot of mosquito bites, and I asked where she had been. She said she had come back from a jungle in the Philippines. She was rebuilding a forest with an NGO, and I told her I had been with an NGO in Afghanistan. We went out the next day and were boyfriend and girlfriend for a year and a half. She'd gone to Waseda University (one of Japan's top private universities). Now she is married to a Norwegian guy and has four kids.

"She was smart and ambitious. Most girls I went out with didn't wear makeup or get dressed up. She just wore jeans and T-shirts. I like people who are natural."

"Why did you guys break up?"

"I wasn't ready for marriage, I guess. It was actually the timing."

"Did she want to get married?"

"Yeah. She didn't said so, but yeah. I messed that up."

The Roppongi girl

"I broke up with my last girlfriend a year and a half ago. She was the only girl I approached on the street and actually went out with. She was working in a club in Roppongi. She was twenty-two or twenty-three, and we dated for about five months. I wanted to be serious, but she wanted to mess around, so I broke up with her. Then six months later, she contacted me saying she wanted to be serious. So we got back together. But she actually wasn't. And I stopped seeing her. And then another six months later, she said she wanted to be serious again, but I didn't get serious this time.

"She dates Japanese guys too. Most girls, after they date a foreigner, they go back to Japanese guys and never date a foreigner again."

The stewardess

"There was a girl who was a stewardess. I saw her on the train. I thought she was really beautiful. She walked next to me from the Inokashira Line (an overground train) all the way downstairs to the Hanzoumon Line (an underground train). She was so beautiful that my heart started to beat fast. I was going to say something to her, but I didn't know what to say. So I thought, *OK, I am going to ask her which one goes to Hanzoumon Station,* because I had a party at an embassy around there. But just as I was about to talk to her, she got a call. I missed the chance.

"Then I went to the party at the embassy. There were usually only politicians, executives, and diplomats at that kind of party. But that girl was there! I thought it was fate. I waved at her. She waved back at me, but then she turned away and linked her arm with a middle-aged man. I thought, *oh, they have that kind of relationship and that's why she's here.* I thought she knew I was at the station because I was constantly paying attention to her, but later, she told me she hadn't recognized me.

"I decided to get some champagne. There was a lady of about sixty standing nearby, and I started talking to her. She was smiling and she was interesting. After a twenty-minute conversation, I asked, 'So do you have company, or are you with the embassy?' She said, 'No, I am with my husband and my daughter. Let me introduce you.' And the girl from the train turned out to be her daughter!

"Then I started dating the girl. Her father owned a big pharmaceutical company. I went out with her for about a year. She was very beautiful, rich, and classy, but maybe a bit selfish. I don't really like selfish girls. I don't want to put too much effort into a relationship. I think she wanted me to make more effort."

Being a Western guy

"A lot of smart girls pretend not to be smart. When they are with a group of foreigners, a girl will be talking and giving opinions, but when a Japanese guy joins a group, suddenly her voice goes up and she'll act cuter and she'll stop being interesting. A few of my friends say, 'It's because if I am bold, guys will say I'm not cute.' A lot of girls don't make the effort to be the best person they can be.

"I was told a number of times by girls that I'm a real gentleman. But it's just the way I treat people. Japanese people don't get the concept of ladies first. It doesn't matter if she's old, young, or cute. If she's a lady, you should treat her like one. A lot of Japanese guys know that treating women well will make them popular, but they only treat well the ones they are interested in. It's actually rude.

"When a Japanese girl likes me, she won't like it if I treat other girls equally well, taking their jackets and carrying their bags. She'll ask, 'Why do you do that for her as well?' On the other hand, when I treat less popular girls well, they will think I'm interested in them. But if they move to Britain, they'll know that everybody is like me and I'm not different."

"Have you gone out with someone completely monolingual?"

"I don't know about very traditional girls, because if they were traditional they wouldn't date a foreigner. But yeah, I have gone out with monolingual girls. I've never spoken English with my girlfriends except for my first girl, and the English girl I dated five years ago. I've only spoken Japanese, so it wouldn't have made a difference if they'd spoken English."

"Do you think being a white guy helps?"

"If you mean getting laid, yeah, it's so much easier because you automatically stand out. If I were a Japanese guy in a room full of Japanese guys, I'd have to be more interesting than the others. But if I'm the only white guy, I'm different. I get more attention immediately. But it also means I attract girls who just want to mess around with guys.

"How do you avoid those superficial girls?"

"I don't think you can tell by the way she looks, so I just find out on a date. If a girl says her hobbies are shopping and karaoke and she wants to get married in the future, that's not a good sign for me.

"Otherwise, no matter how cute she is, if she never tries to pay and just lets me pay, I'll never date her again. I won't let her pay in the end, but there are many girls who don't even say 'thank you.' Just because they are cute, they think they can get away with that. I've blown girls off a few times even though they went home with me and we had sex that night. They would say, 'Hope to see you soon,' but I would say, 'No, you didn't even say "Thank you" when I bought those drinks.' They would say, 'But everybody does that in Japan,' so I would say, 'No, it's just cute girls.'"

"Any advice for guys who want serious relationships?"

"Don't find them in Roppongi. Actually, a lot of girls are trying to find guys who are not spoiled yet and want serious relationships. Those guys who remain in Japan for more than one year get arrogant. So girls want to meet somebody who is not used to Japan. But the question is, where do you meet these girls? If you look for someone among your friends' friends, or ask your friend's girlfriend to introduce someone, you are more likely to find someone serious.

"But it's difficult to meet the right girl who is international and professional. I'm forty-one, but I don't want someone just to have a baby with. I want her to truly like me. And it's hard."

After the interview

When I was about to finish the interview, James got a call from a Japanese girl. He said she was a friend he'd met through a mutual friend.

He picked up the phone and said in Japanese, "You're early. I thought we were meeting at nine."

That was when I understood why he had said he could only stay until nine pm. He was meeting that girl.

But next, he said something quite unexpected:

"So, my friend is already here. Either she can come and join us, or I can probably go and meet her there. What do you think?"

Apparently, he was sort of inviting me to join them. I thought he was going to meet her alone. I became curious.

"Well, she can come. I won't mind," I said.

"It's been a long time," the Japanese girl said to James.

"I said hi to her, and we introduced ourselves rather awkwardly. She sat at the table.

After she joined us, James became more talkative and attentive. He seemed to be trying to make the conversation interesting and continuous. We switched to Japanese almost entirely, and the girl became the center of attention.

At the same time, he didn't forget to include me in the conversation. Some guys completely forget about other guys once they start talking to a girl, but that wasn't his style. He has good social skills.

He started flirting with her, touching her lightly on her arms and thighs. He poured wine for her. (For the record, he poured wine for me, too.) He fed her cheese, picking up pieces and putting them into her mouth. The girl looked at him with dreamy eyes.

Suddenly, I had an idea: asking her about dating in Japan. It was a perfect occasion. I had a white guy and a Japanese girl at the same table. The only problem was that such question might not be appropriate in this situation.

But I decided to go ahead.

"Do you have any opinion about intercultural dating in Japan?" I asked.

The question made her visibly uncomfortable. "Uh..." she searched for words. There was a long pause.

She turned to James and say, 'Well... I don't really know how to act in this situation.' James carefully explained to her about the interview. He was very helpful, but at the same time, he didn't pressure her to answer.

I wasn't giving up yet. "OK, for example, some Western guys think that Japanese girls are easy. What's your opinion on this?"

This question rendered her even more uncomfortable.

"No comment," she said after a long pause.

Then the guy showed up.

He was an old British guy and appeared out of nowhere. He was either very drunk or high, and was staggering along the street. He was wearing a T-shirt and casual trousers. But the most unusual thing was that he was holding a bouquet of flowers.

"Move away, cunt!" he said to me. I was confused. It was downright rude, but it was so out of context that I wasn't sure if he was serious or joking.

"Move away, cunt!" he repeated. It didn't sound threatening. He could barely speak clearly.

"Let me get you a chair," James said calmly. He went inside and brought back a chair. The guy sat down.

"Who are your flowers for?" James asked.

"They are for my mother," the guy said. But then he noticed the Japanese girl and changed his mind.

"Here, they are for you," he said and handed the flowers to her. "You are beautiful, so I am giving them to you," he said.

The girl was confused. She just half-smiled awkwardly. She didn't know what to do, but eventually accepted the flowers reluctantly.

"Are you two together?" the guy asked.

The question put the Japanese girl and James in a very awkward position. They briefly looked at each other but didn't say anything.

Eventually, the guy left. "I wonder if he will be able to get home in that state," we said to each other.

When we left the bar, it was nearly eleven. I was taking the train home. I had assumed that the girl was coming to the station with me because I thought she needed to go home too.

But when I said goodbye, the girl didn't move. She was staying. So I said goodbye to her as well, and left for the station.

Discussions

You might have come across white guys bragging about how easy it is to get girls in Japan, and some of James' stories overlap with theirs. There are often common elements in these stories: Roppongi and Western bars.

Roppongi can easily be called the most un-Japanese place in Japan. Its vibrant nightlife caters chiefly to international people, unlike other areas of Tokyo. Western bars—which are rare in Japan—are the norm in Roppongi.

What I'd like to underline is that Tokyo—and Japan—is much more than Roppongi and Western bars. Sometimes, I have the impression that these bars are overrepresented when it comes to stories of Tokyo and Japan in the English-speaking community. But these places are atypical in many ways, and the stories should be understood in this context.

James talks about girls who break up with foreign guys and immediately marry Japanese guys upon turning twenty-seven. He says that they then start dating foreign guys again after a few years of marriage. Again, I don't think they represent the majority of Japanese women, but I find that there's something cultural in this anecdote.

Japanese people tend to view marriage as a family institution rather than the crystallization of love. At the same time, marriage has a very important place in Japanese society and people often face a lot of pressure to get married before a certain age (many people think thirty is the critical point). Japanese women in particular seem to have to deal with the pressure that often comes from their parents and people around them.

We can explain James' example in this context. The Japanese women in his example marry Japanese guys before they turn thirty, because they want to achieve a good social standing. However, they don't expect much romance in their marriage; instead, they look for it elsewhere. They might think—even though it's not necessarily true—that non-Japanese citizens are less likely to get serious because they'll eventually leave and thus, not become a threat to their marriage.

James also meets girls outside bars and Roppongi. For example, he talks to girls on the train. In my opinion, this doesn't always work. (Oddly enough, I have talked to people on the train in Tokyo.) But it's not impossible. The key is to find a reason to open your mouth. Asking for directions is one way, or you could comment on what they are reading. But if they don't want to talk to you, don't take it personally. It's not you. It's Tokyo.

9. Kala—The black girl's mission: "Get That Guy"

How she orchestrated a plan to get a cute guy in the student building

Mᴀʀᴄʜ 2004, Gᴇᴏʀɢɪᴀ. Kᴀʟᴀ ᴡᴀs home after a long day at work. She was going to talk with her long-distance Japanese boyfriend on Yahoo Messenger. They had met when she was in Japan three years ago and since her return to the US, it had become their habit to chat online.

She turned on the computer, expecting him to be online. However, she only found a message that he had left. "Sorry, something came up. I can't be online tonight," he wrote.

"Fine, I'm tired anyway. I'm just going to go to bed," she thought.

Just as she was about to go to bed, she heard a knock on the door. *Who the hell is that?*, she wondered. It was almost ten pm, too late for a visitor.

"Who is it?" she said.

"Hey, it's Shinji," said the visitor.

She was confused. Shinji was her boyfriend, but she wasn't expecting him at all. He was supposed to be in Japan. Besides, her neighborhood wasn't exactly tourist-friendly.

She opened the door and indeed, there he was, a Japanese guy right in her predominantly black neighborhood. She screamed in surprise. She went back in, sprinkled some water on her face, and then went back to talk to him.

That night, he proposed to her.

"How did he propose?"

"That's a good question, but I don't remember. Just, you know, something like, 'Will you marry me?'"

"Well, he must have said something."

"Yeah. He said something because I said something." She laughed. "I just remember I was so happy. It was a complete surprise. It was about ten-thirty at night. Can you believe that? He took the bus to my neighborhood."

Kala seemed to be a perfectly normal American girl. Growing up in Ohio with her single mother and sisters, she seemed to have led a pretty ordinary American life. Until she came to Japan.

The high school guy

"Did you date any guys in high school?"

"I dated this guy in the last year of my high school for about three years. We lived one street away from each other. He was two years older.

"What was his background?"

"He was black. The area where I grew up was ninety percent black. Working-class neighborhood."

"What did you guys do on a date?"

"When we had money, we went out to a restaurant. I loved going to his house. His grandma's cooking was so good. I always tried to be there around dinnertime. She'd say, 'Since you're here, do you want to eat?' I'd say, 'Well, you know, if you have enough?' She was always nice to me. She made stir fries. I'd never had stir fries before."

The homestay

When Kala was seventeen, she decided to go on a summer study abroad program.

"When Americans do a homestay, they usually choose to do it in a European country. But I wanted to go to a completely different country. I wanted to do the opposite of what everybody was doing. So I thought, 'What's the opposite of everything?' That's how I came up with Japan. We needed to raise money selling candy bars to join the program."

She lived in Kyushu, an island half the size of Ireland in the southwestern part of Japan. She was there for six weeks.

"We lived close to Space World. I could see the roller coaster from my bedroom, and for a teenager, that was heaven. We went to Space World. My host sister was one year younger than me, so I went to her high school. I wore her uniform. I had the best time there. And my host mother's food was really, really good. I loved UFO noodles. I thought they were the best. You know, in America, noodles come in packages, but there they were in this special UFO container.

"We went to the hot spring in Beppu. My host family said, 'We're going to a hot spring,' and I said, 'Great!' And they said, 'Naked, OK?' But I didn't quite understand what they meant. Then when we got there everybody started taking off their clothes and I thought, *uh oh, what's happening?* Then I thought, *well, I'm in Japan and no one's going to know about this,* and I took my clothes off, because if you don't do it, you'll miss out. I don't like to miss out."

The Japanese teacher

Since the homestay, Kala had always wanted to come back to Japan, and the opportunity came up pretty soon. In her third year of college, she did one semester in Nagoya, a medium-sized city in central Japan.

"In my opinion, Nagoya is not good if you are a student, because it's a very expensive city. If you are a poor student, you can't do anything. Tokyo has more free stuff."

"Did you date anybody?"

"No. But I fell in love with my teacher. I developed a crush on him, but he had a girlfriend. He taught Japanese, although he taught level 5 and I was in level 4. I tried to get into level 5, but not because of him! It was because I thought my Japanese was very good. But I was really struggling, so they said, 'You can try level 4.'"

"Was he the first Asian guy you were interested in?"

"Yeah. In high school, there were definitely no Asian people. A friend came to visit me in Japan a few years ago, first time in Asia. I met her at Narita Airport. She got off the plane and said, 'Why are there so many Asian people?' I said, 'But you are in Asia!' That was so funny. I hadn't had any exposure to Asian people before I came here."

The awesome guy

Her experience in Nagoya convinced her that she wanted to live in Japan longer, so she decided to apply for the JET program. She was placed in Kagoshima, on the southwestern tip of the island of Kyushu. Little did she know she would be meeting her future husband there.

"Even though many foreigners were interested in Japan, our Japanese wasn't up to a level where we could have regular conversations in it. So we started a Let's-Speak-Japanese

Club to improve our Japanese. We held club meetings in a dormitory in an international student building at the university. Many people came to the club. The Japanese came, foreign students came, and JET teachers came.

"One day, we were sitting there talking, and there was this guy with a great haircut. He smiled and walked upstairs. I asked, 'Who was that guy?' They said, 'I think he lives here.' I wanted to meet him.

"Our conversation completely changed. We started a mission: 'Get That Guy.' I got all my friends together and they each had a different role. I was like, 'OK, you do this, and you do that.' One of my friends invited him to the Let's-Speak-Japanese Club. My Japanese friends gave me tips to get a Japanese guy. They also helped me with my Japanese. I'll never forget that.

"He ended up joining the club and we would talk about everything. Then, I had a plan. I said to him, 'I heard you were a tutor, so maybe you can help me with my Japanese?' He said, 'Yeah, sure.'

"In fact, he was what we call an 'RA' in American English. RA is resident assistant. When you live in a dormitory, there's a person who is in charge of each floor. But they used the word 'tutor' for this, so when I heard 'tutor,' I thought it meant someone who helped you with schoolwork.

"So one day, I brought something I needed help with. I didn't need any help. I just wanted to meet him. He tried to explain stuff, but he wasn't really that good at it, so I was thinking, *how is he a tutor?* It was just the two of us. That was the first time I talked to him one on one.

"There was an international party for foreign students and everyone was invited, and of course he was there helping, setting up things. I went to the party with one of my guy friends.

"We saw him. He said 'Hi' and I said 'Hi.' Then we saw this girl coming up to him and putting her hand on his back. I was shocked. I said, 'What's happening?' and my friend said, 'I'm sorry, but that's his girlfriend. In Japan, if a girl acts like that, it means she's his girlfriend.'

"After that, we went to a bar and I asked, 'What can I do?' My friend said, 'Maybe you can get to know him better. What is he interested in?'

I said, 'Well, I think he's interested in football.'

'Do you know anything about football?'

'Not really.'

'Do you know Pele?'

'What is a Pele?'

"You know, we don't watch football in America! But I started learning about football.

"I invited him to a Thanksgiving party. I'd had a few parties at my place before, but this time, I decided to have a Thanksgiving party so I could invite him.

"Many of my friends came and he also came. I made him a special map to help him get to my place. He made sweet potato balls. They tasted just OK and I noticed that not many people were eating them. I thought he might be sad at this, so I started eating them. I said, 'Thank you for bringing these. They are really good.' When he was leaving, there were still some left. I said, 'Can I keep these?'

"Then at a different party, I finally asked him if he still had a girlfriend. I was really nervous. It turned out he had broken up with her. After that, we started going out together.

"We would go somewhere to eat or hang out with friends. He would come to the Let's-Speak-Japanese Club. I went to his house for dinner and spent time with his family. They were all so nice. One of his sisters was one of my students in the high school I was teaching at. I had found out they were brother and sister because their last name was kind of rare.

I was at the school and checking the tests and I thought, *oh she has the same name that he does.*

"Actually, they remember things better than I do. Apparently I took a melon to their house. They still say, 'That was so nice.' His mom's cooking was so good. I think I made lasagna and that was the first time they had it. Everybody loved the lasagna. After that, it became me equals lasagna."

"Did you guys speak English or Japanese?"

"Both, but at that time, probably mostly English. He had studied and lived in Australia for three or four years. At first, he was there for a study abroad program, and then he went for a working holiday. After he came back from Australia, instead of living at home, he wanted to live in an international community. He had had a really good experience in Australia."

After the JET program was over, she had to go back to the States.

"I left Kagoshima in 2001 and went back to the States. I got a job. I got a car. Eventually I got a house. During that time, we would see each other once or twice a year. I went to Kagoshima the next year, and then the year after that he came to the States. At the time, there wasn't the technology we have now, so we used Yahoo Messenger. That was our date.

"And then the year after that we went to Hawaii. Hawaii was interesting because I just knew it. We had been dating for about three years, so I knew we were going to get married. Who the fuck goes to Hawaii and never gets married? I said to myself, 'OK, it's happening.'

"We had a great time in Hawaii. Now, day after day, I was like, 'OK, when is it happening?' It was Thanksgiving. We were at the mall. We saw a movie, and after the movie, we got to talk. He said, 'I don't think I can propose right now.' I thought, *what the...?* I had got all these new clothes and my hair done. Who goes to Hawaii and doesn't get engaged?

"He was twenty-six. He said, 'I can't offer you anything right now,' because he was just starting his job. But I didn't need him to offer me anything except marriage! I was like, 'You know what? Just whatever.'

"I went back to the States and he went back to Kagoshima. Then, the next April, he started his job in Tokyo and moved to Chiba. We continued to date using Yahoo Messenger.

"I was going through a phase. I cut my hair. I just didn't know what was happening with the relationship, so I started thinking, *well, maybe this isn't going to work.*

"It was the end of November when we went to Hawaii and his birthday was in December, so I got him a suit as a birthday present. He just had started working, so I wanted to give him a nice suit.

"One day, the next spring, we were supposed to have a date on Yahoo messenger. I get on the computer and he sends a message saying, 'Sorry, something came up. I can't be online tonight.' I remember I was so tired that night. So I said, 'Fine, I'm tired anyway. I'm just going to go to bed.' When I was getting ready to go to bed, I heard a knock on the door. I asked, 'Who is that?' It was almost ten o'clock. The person said, 'It's Shinji.' I opened the door and was surprised. I closed the door, ran to my bathroom, sprayed some water on my face, and came back and let him in. He was wearing the suit I gave him! Then he asked me to marry him. It was a complete surprise. I don't remember exactly what he said. I just remember I was so happy. That was four years after we had first met."

"What kind of person is he?"

"Cute. He has a kind of boyish personality. He's very intelligent in some areas, like math and science. I'm not so good. I used to ask him to do some math and he would do it in the air. I would just sit there and think, *wow, he's so cool.*

"He's a surfer. He loves sports. He plays basketball. He loves football. Sometime I joke about it saying that I'm number four in his life. Number one is his surfboard. Number two is his Japanese national football team. Number three is maybe his basketball. And number four is me. Yay! He gets pretty mad when I say that. He says, 'You're number one, you're number one!'

"I shouldn't say this, but my mom came to visit me the last year of the JET program. She loved him. She said he was great. We went to Chinan, which is the samurai area in Kagoshima. They had this samurai house and we took a picture of him and me. We were just sitting there, but if you look at the picture, it looks like he was touching my butt even though he wasn't. So I said, 'Oh, this is a really good picture. I'm going to send it to my grandmother.' And he said, 'No, no, you can't send it, because she will think I'm a man of touching butt.' 'Man of touching butt' is really cute English. It's not exactly correct, but the meaning is very obvious. He's really cute."

"How's your married life?"

"Difficult… People always say you have to work at a marriage and I think that's very, very true. It's not what you see in the movies."

"What did you have to work at?"

"It wasn't so much the marriage. It was becoming a housewife. I was working in the States, but I quit my job to come here. In Japan, I didn't have a job, which in a way was good, but in another way it was very lonely. I had a house and a car in the States. But here I had no car or job. At his first company, he was working until twelve pm. I was at home by myself for most of the day. I went out to do grocery shopping, but that was it."

"Did you talk about it with your husband?"

"Not so much. He was too busy. The first year at his company, his bosses were assholes."

Her husband's company decided to send him to Chile for a few months. But Kala had to stay. She went back to the States and when he came back, they started living in Chigasaki, near the ocean.

"How was your social life in Chigasaki?"

"It was better than in Chiba. But the first year, there wasn't much of it because there was this surfing culture and I didn't feel like I belonged to it. There were surfer girls there who think Hawaii is the best place in the world."

"He chose to live there because of surfing?"

"His number one love, so yeah! Chigasaki was a nice place. We were there for three years."

"Were you still a housewife?"

"For the first year, yes. But then I got a job at the university, and I made friends through work. I joined MIJ which means 'Married in Japan.' It's for foreign women living in Japan that are in relationships with Japanese men. That was a Yahoo group. They still do it. I met a really good friend there, and we're still good friends. But she's not in a relationship with that Japanese guy anymore. He was a nice guy. He was also a surfer, so he and my husband would go surfing together."

"How did your job affect your married life?"

"At first not so much, but after a while it became difficult. I still made up a lunch box in the morning and made dinner at night. He woke up earlier because he had to go to Tokyo from Chigasaki and it would take an hour and half.

"So I woke up in the morning, made sure he had breakfast, made our lunches for later, and then I got ready. I packed my breakfast and I went to work. I did that for two years. But the second year, the work situation became very, very stressful and I was working very long hours. He was worried because I was so stressed. He could tell that I was losing weight and didn't have any energy left. That was a hard time. But after that, we found out that his company was sending him to South America again, and we were going to Peru. We were like, 'Banzai! Sayonara, suckers!'

"The company said they wanted him to go to Peru to run the office there. They said we were going to be there for around four years. I loved Lima. The food was so good, and of course, I learned Spanish. I went to a language school, so I made friends there from places like Indonesia, Korea, Poland, and Belgium. My best friend at the time was Indonesian.

"Then something happened, and the company decided they wanted him back in Japan. We came back after ten months.

"I lived near Yokohama station for about three years. It was very nice. My husband's company provided us with an apartment.

"The social life was better now. I still had a friend who lived in Chigasaki, even though she and her boyfriend had broken up. The company owned the apartment building, so I met some of the other ladies. I had a friend in Numazu. It was easy to get there by train because the train went straight from Yokohama Station to Numazu. I enjoyed living in Yokohama. It was easy access to anywhere. And if I got a part-time job, you know it was so easy to get there."

Then Kala moved to her current place near Chinatown. Chinatown in Yokohama is much more touristy than Chinatowns in the States. There are a lot of nice restaurants and cafés.

"I've met many people since I have started living here because I joined a lot of groups and meetups. I met an

American girl at the Spanish meetup. We went to Odaiba for Cinco de Mayo together. Her sister and I finished university together. We were in the same year. Actually, we all went to the same university. She is one year behind me. Isn't it funny that I met her in Japan? I had never met her before. It's a small world.

"I made some Japanese friends working at the university. Actually, one of my very good friends lives near me. But she's leaving for Canada. I haven't made many Japanese friends, actually. Well, this is due to a cultural difference because, for example, there's a lady in the building next to me, and so we use the same station. One day I was coming home and I saw her. We were both black ladies and I said, 'Wow, I like your hair,' and she said, 'I like yours too!' We started talking and we walked home together and talked some more. She's my friend now. But I find that we cannot do that with Japanese people. I definitely had more Japanese friends in Kagoshima."

"What is the hardest thing about your marriage?"

"Communication. I communicate a lot. If I think of something, I probably say it. If I'm hungry, I don't hesitate to say I'm hungry. He wouldn't say he's hungry. If he's hungry, he comes to the kitchen and starts asking me questions. If I'm cooking, he will say, 'Do you need some help?' I use my 'automatic translator' to understand that he actually means 'I'm hungry.' Or sometimes when he says 'Do you need help?' it really means that he feels he *should* help, but really he doesn't want to."

"How do you guys decide what to eat?"

"I decide. If he wants what I want, he will say 'OK.' If he doesn't, he'll say 'sss' and then I have to use my automatic translator again and figure out that he doesn't want that."

"How about going on a vacation?"

"Usually I say I want to go somewhere. And he'll say 'sss' or 'mmm?' Very rarely does he say 'Yeah, I want to go there!' For example, for many, many years I've been saying I want to go skiing in Zaou. And always says, 'sss' or 'mmm' or 'arr.' Just many noises! But finally this year, I said, 'I'm going to Zaou' and he said, 'OK, let's go.' Well, he is not excited about going, but he knows if he doesn't say OK, I'm going to go crazy, and he doesn't want a crazy wife."

"How do you know what he's really thinking?"

"You tell me! This is a great mystery. I'd like to know what he's thinking. Sometimes I just look at him and wonder what he's thinking. I even ask him, 'What are you thinking?' and he doesn't know! Or he just says he doesn't know."

"Is he a good listener?"

"Sometimes? If I say something while a football game is on, he doesn't hear me. He's concentrating a hundred percent. Or it depends on the topic. I mean, we are interested in different things. I'm interested in human relationships, but he is more interested in sports. If you are not talking about sports, then he only has so much interest. I am talking, talking, and talking, but his mind is somewhere else."

"Does he talk about his personal problems?"

"No."

"Do you want him to talk about these things?"

"Oh, that would be great. Do you know how to get him to talk? That would be awesome. That's an awesome question.

"But overall, I don't think that intercultural or interracial relationships are any different from any other relationships. You have to work at them anyway. You know, if you have an idea that 'I'm going to meet some great foreigner and it's going be so great,' I don't think that's a realistic expectation. I know that some people purposefully want to marry a foreigner, but I don't think that's good. Everybody is welcome to be in a relationship with whomever they like.

But you shouldn't think that marrying a foreigner is going to be any better than marrying somebody from your own country. You still have to work on the relationship."

Kala seems to be enjoying her life in Yokohama. She was chatting with the staff in the café where I was interviewing her. Apparently, she is a regular. She laughed out loud a lot during the interview and when she didn't remember something, she just said, 'I don't remember' and moved on to the next subject. She isn't an over-thinker. She doesn't worry about things unnecessarily.

Discussions

Kala's *automatic translator* is a very interesting concept. It's no secret that Japanese people use a lot of nonverbal cues to express themselves. Kala seems to have gotten better at understanding these cues during the course of dealing with her husband.

There was an episode in Hawaii where her husband said he couldn't propose to her right away because he had just started his job. This can be better understood from a cultural perspective. As I mentioned earlier, Japanese people tend to view marriage as a family institution. Her husband might have wanted to be sure that he could support the marriage financially; he needed a concrete plan. He might have wanted to be responsible in his own way.

Another interesting aspect of her story is that she actively approached her husband. I think her strategy was perfect. She tried to get to know him first by inviting him to her Japanese club. Then she invited him to private parties to get closer to him. Her approach was indirect, but I think it would work well with a lot of Japanese guys. Personally, I don't mind being approached in a direct way, but I've heard some Japanese guys say Western girls are "too aggressive." But I'm pretty sure most Japanese guys would be totally OK with being approached by girls, as long as it's done in a prudent manner (Japanese guys can be quite self-conscious).

10. Sean—The rules of Japanese gays

The hidden world of Japanese gay guys

THERE IS A PLACE CALLED *Ni-chome* in Tokyo. *Ni-chome* is in Shinjuku, where the busiest train station in Japan is. It is known as a gay town, and a lot of gay guys flock there at night.

Sean, a British guy, didn't know much about this when he arrived in Japan.

"I didn't have much knowledge about Japan. I just knew I wanted to try something different. I thought it would be really cool to learn Japanese and I thought if I went to Japan, I would just pick it up, which I now know was a very naïve idea. If I wanted to learn Spanish, going to Spain would be a good idea because people would talk to you and teach you. But in Japan, that just doesn't happen.

"My first impression of Japan was quite negative, actually. But it had nothing to do with Japan or Japanese people. It was because of the treatment I got at the company I was working for. The plane trip from London to Narita was organized by the company. There were about ten of us. Everyone was going to a different place, and I was the only person who was going to Kanagawa (a prefecture near Tokyo). The person who met us at the airport handed me a ticket and said, 'You are taking the Narita Express and a guy will meet you at your stop at the end.'

"Two hours later, I was in Fujisawa (a city in Kanagawa prefecture). My first impression was that I had made a terrible mistake. I thought they'd posted me in the middle of nowhere. When I looked at the map, I thought Fujisawa was quite near Tokyo.

"There were already two people living in the apartment, but they weren't home. One of them had written a letter to me. It was on the table and it said, 'Please tell the person standing next to you that your room is not habitable.' We opened the door and it was really terrible. They ended up having to move me.

"My experience with that company from the very beginning to the end was bad. I thought maybe it was just me, but it wasn't. The majority of the people I worked with couldn't wait to leave. One day, a guy I worked with didn't go to work and just went to the airport instead. He didn't even call the company. He called me to tell me he was at the airport and said, 'I'll see you somewhere down the road.' He actually ended up coming back to Japan for a holiday, but he just couldn't go back to work."

The company in question was a very famous English language school in Japan. They were extremely well-known because they advertised their school aggressively. They had a bad reputation because of the way they treated students and teachers. Eventually, they went bankrupt.

"Fujisawa at the time was very nice and foreigner-friendly. All the teachers who worked around the area lived there. There were a few foreign bars and they would get pretty busy almost daily. We would end up there most nights.

Because most people realized that the job itself wasn't good, they thought, 'I'm only here for a year, so I'm just going to have as much fun as I can.' It was basically meeting as many people as you could for casual sex, drinking, and partying every night.

"On our days off, people would always head into Tokyo. It was frustrating at first because my days off were Wednesday and Thursday. If you lived in London, that wouldn't be a problem, because there's always things going on. But in Shinjuku, it's not like that. The boss at the school would say, 'Just pretend that Wednesday is Saturday.' But it didn't work that way.

"Eventually, somebody left the school and his days off were Sunday and Monday. So I managed to pinch his shift. I still worked on Saturday, but that wasn't a big deal for me. I finished at five, and as a ritual every week, I would go home as quickly as possible, get changed, and take the JR train to Shinjuku. I had a friend who lived there and I would crash at his place. I wouldn't be back in Fujisawa until Monday. I pretty much did that every week."

Rules of the game

"The dating scene around *Ni-chome* is pretty competitive. There are two scenes: the Japanese guys who hang out there were either *nihon-sen* (exclusively dating Japanese) or *gai-sen* (exclusively dating foreigners). There are around 200 bars in *Ni-chome* and about 95% are only for Japanese guys. If you are a foreigner, it's quite difficult to even enter those bars. In the UK, this would be classed as a form of discrimination, but in Japan, it's a form of what I would call classification. It makes it easier for people to make choices if you know where you are going, so I know why Japanese people like that style. In bars where the guys are into foreign guys, they will match up very quickly. Some of those relationships are still going. The longest I can think of is ten years.

"If you think about the scene for foreigners, there are probably about five different places you can go to. Everybody knows everyone's names and it's always the same people who go there. But the proportion is something like 80% Japanese and 20% foreigners. There aren't enough foreigners, so it becomes very competitive.

"Of course, the Japanese guys are all very nice to us, but they are very aggressive to each other. As soon as you get into anything that is considered to be a relationship, your Japanese partner will segregate you from the crowd. They will try to remove you from that scene. *Gai-sen* Japanese guys consider *Ni-chome* to be only a place where you find a boyfriend. Once in a relationship, they won't go back, because Japanese guys will try to break up their relationship and steal their boyfriend.

"I got myself into quite a bit of trouble by being in the wrong place at the wrong time. When I was in a previous relationship, I was constantly getting into trouble by breaking these social interaction rules. 'Don't sit next to a person,' 'Don't engage him in a conversation or accept anything from him,' or 'If somebody offers you a drink, politely say no.'

"We would go out and seemingly everything was fine. But when we went back home we would have a huge argument or fight about the list of 'crimes' I had committed."

The *Ni-chome* guy

"I'd always been fairly successful meeting people in bars in Japan. I'm not even sure why. Everybody always complained that they went out with the intention of meeting people and nothing ever happened. But that had never been an issue for me. One day, I was in a bar in *Ni-chome* and a guy came over to see me. That was actually typical in *Ni-chome*. If a Japanese guy sees a foreigner by himself, it's a bit like finding a piece of gold in a river. You need to grab it quickly.

"I was quite lucky that this guy was charming and good-looking. He'd had a British boyfriend before and I think he had a TOEIC score of about 800 (a standardized English test popular in Japan; 990 is a perfect score). I was taking Japanese lessons, but my Japanese wasn't good enough to chat somebody up in a bar.

"We exchanged numbers and agreed to meet the following week. It was the official first date. We met in a bar.

"But I thought it was too soon to be in a relationship. I'd been in a relationship for almost two years before I came to Japan and I'd only been in Japan for three months. Also, I thought I was going to leave in a year. If I got into in a relationship, it would be another one where you had to say goodbye at the airport. I wasn't going to let that happen this time.

"But I ended up in a relationship with him and stayed for four years.

"The beginning of the relationship was pretty rocky. He basically gave me an ultimatum saying, 'Look, you either take it seriously or you don't. And if you don't, you'll never speak to me again.' It was the first time that anybody had said that to me.

"I said, 'Well, I'm going to have to think about it.' I did think, and in the end I said OK. We agreed to make it official. Part of the deal was not to speak to any of the people I was with. It was him or them. So I had to delete numbers from my phone, say goodbye, and if I saw them, I would have to ignore them. To be honest with you, I didn't do that fully. Not that I was like screwing around, but I just couldn't accept that. It seemed to be a very childish thing to do. I would meet people just for a conversation from time to time without telling anybody."

"Were your friends understanding?"

"To them it was just normal. They knew the rules."

"What was it about him that made you want to be exclusive?"

"He was actually a very helpful person, and also we seemed to have quite similar interests. But I'm not sure if he created some of the interests just to start the relationship. The only two things we really had in common were drinking and music. The music part was fine, but the drinking sometimes got out of hand, to the point where we had to leave a place.

"One thing you have in Japan that you don't have in the UK is *nomi-hodai* (all you can drink), because basically in the UK, it would be too dangerous. All the bars in *Ni-chome* are *nomi-hodai*. And it's very cheap. It's only 1000 yen (about $10) in some places. That got a lot of people into a lot of trouble. At that time in the early 2000s, the expat community in *Ni-chome* was quite big. That in combination with *nomi-hodai* resulted some pretty intense fights.

"There was one bar at the corner of a street in the middle of *Ni-chome* where you could sit outside. That bar was very popular in summertime. There was a small table, a bench, and a couple of small chairs. Two Japanese guys were sitting on the bench and a foreign guy sat down opposite them. I sat down on the bench and my boyfriend sat down next to me and we were talking to each other just casually. The foreign guy started talking to me. Then two Japanese guys started talking to me and before I knew it, everybody was in the conversation. When that finished, we decided to go home.

"One thing we used to do was get some drinks on the way back home. So we stopped at an Indian restaurant where we had a really big fight. He accused me of ruining the whole night by interfering too much with the two Japanese guys' attempt to catch the foreign guy. I was completely knocked sideways by this accusation. I thought it had been a completely innocent conversation. He said no. It was obvious to him that one of the Japanese guys was interested in the foreigner. I'd now ruined the evening for that guy because I kind of broke up that communication. He had also probably memorized my face and name and he was going to say bad things about me to other Japanese people, which I think probably did happen. I mean, at the time, I thought it was a crazy thing to suggest, but as I learned more about *Ni-chome*, I can agree with him on that.

"The rule is basically that if you see a Japanese guy and a foreigner talking, you should walk away. I shouldn't even have sat down. And don't break into somebody's conversation. When they started talking to each other, I should have gotten up and moved away. These are the social interaction rules you can only learn by breaking them.

"What started out as him complaining to me escalated to the point where we were almost shouting at each other. Then I just walked out of the restaurant. We got back to his apartment and continued shouting until I stormed out. We actually lived near each other. I could walk to my apartment in ten minutes. And when something like that happened, I would always walk back.

"I shared an apartment with two foreign guys and it was in a big building. My room was next to the front door and the window was inside-facing. The air-conditioning unit was the type that fitted inside the window. You had to open the window to switch it on. But that meant you could just slide the window open from the outside. So whenever we had a fight and I walked home, he would come to my apartment early the next morning, open the window, and force me to wake up. And then he would say, 'I'm sorry.' This cycle repeated each time.

"We'd been in a relationship for three years, but it really shouldn't have lasted more than a year, because the two years in the end were just a repetition of that. Towards the very end, this type of thing would happen every week until it got to the point where I thought I was never going to get out of the relationship.

"That was part of my motivation for leaving. At the time, the Japanese government would give you a three-year visa, and I still had two years remaining because I had just renewed it. But I wanted to go away. I still had the option to come back if I want to.

"I decided to go to New York, and then back to London before deciding whether to go back to Tokyo. It would give me enough time to officially break up the relationship. I bought the ticket and said, 'Our relationship as friends will be much better. I'm going. It's not a permanent move. I'll come back. But you and I are probably not going to be in a relationship when I come back. When I'm gone, you'll have to think about that.'

"What was his reaction?"

"Denial. For the first couple of months while I was away, he just wouldn't acknowledge the fact that it was finished. He would send me stuff from Japan like DVDs or food products. Eventually, I wrote a letter back and said, 'It's very nice of you to send the stuff. But you have to stop because we are not together anymore.'

"When I came back, he fell into the old pattern saying, 'Let's go out drinking together.' I knew he wanted to talk about something with me. That was a kind of code. After an hour he said, 'So are we back together?' I said, 'No, we're not.' I think that was when he finally realized it was over."

"I had to stay with a friend for a while because getting an apartment in Japan wasn't easy. I needed a guarantor. It was kind of a transitional period I think. My ex-boyfriend helped me find an apartment and guaranteed the rent. I said to him, 'You know you are doing this as a friend, right?' And he said that was OK.

"There were a couple of incidents after that where he got angry about something. And it was kind of liberating. I said, 'I'm sorry you're angry or upset about whatever it is. I'm sure you can talk to your other friends. It's not appropriate to talk to me about this.' After that happened, things became much better."

"What's the difference between Japanese guys dating other Japanese guys versus dating foreign guys?"

"I think there was a certain liberation associated with foreign guys because a lot of the conformity has to do with the Japanese relationship style. I know Japanese guys who are in a relationship with each other and that's always much more stressful. They say they have so many work commitments and things they have to do. They are not allowed to know each other's family, whereas as soon as you date a foreign guy, you will get to know all of the family. I get the feeling that Japanese gay guys never fully open up to each other."

"But they still have strict rules with foreign guys, right?"

"Absolutely. So that's the paradox. A Japanese guy who likes foreigners feels liberated in some way, but still wants foreign guys to conform to the Japanese style. Also, I think their inability to explain the rules makes relationships bad. But if they were open about the rules and conformity, it would be too scary for foreign guys and they just wouldn't date them. I even met quite a few foreign guys in Japan who said, 'I don't date Japanese guys because there are too many rules.'"

The online guy

"I hadn't rented an apartment by myself until I was thirty-three. Up until that time, I'd always shared apartments with other people who were around the same age as me. In 2006, I moved back to Japan and eventually got an apartment. I said, 'OK, I'm not in a relationship. I have my own place. I can just do what I want.' But I met somebody six months after that.

"It was the first time ever I met somebody on a dating site and it turned into a relationship. I hadn't had much success with online dating. Now that dating has moved online, people easily change their minds. They agree to do something and suddenly the plan is changed. To me, that was always too much trouble.

"I noticed on his profile that he used to live in London. I thought, *this is somebody who understands my culture.* He was younger than me by eight years. I send him a message. Eventually, he said, 'Let's meet up' and we met up for coffee. We ended up going for a drink. We exchanged numbers but at the time, I wasn't particularly motivated to date.

"We ended up bumping into each other again. He wanted to go on a date again. I reluctantly agreed and then we went on dates a couple of times.

"We ended up making it official pretty much three or four months later. I asked him to make it official, but he was just about to ask me. So if I hadn't said anything at the time, he would have said it. He immediately said yes. He wasn't like, 'I want to think about it.' My experiences in the past had always been, 'Let me think about it at least.'

"It was the first relationship where we had nothing in common. I've never really had criteria for meeting people casually, but for a relationship, I'd always thought we should have something in common. But this one, we had nothing. But I thought maybe I should take a chance. So I did.

"After we'd been dating a year and a half, I had to think about renewing my apartment lease. I asked him, 'Do you want to move in together?' and he said yes. We ended up living together in Tokyo for about three years."

"Does he also have strict rules?"

"No. For a lot of the guys that I know, their first experience with dating is *Ni-chome*. All their reactions and their way of thinking come from that starting point. But my partner had a relationship with a woman in Japan and had never been to *Ni-chome*. Actually, he didn't come out until he was in London. So his starting point is London. He knows how people interact in a different way. For him, the *Ni-chome* situation is quite weird and stressful. It's hard for him to understand. In fact, I understand better than he does.

"The majority of his Japanese friends are straight. I think that makes a difference. For my ex-boyfriend whom I dated for three years, his first experience of any social interaction outside school was *Ni-chome,* and that was where all his friends came from. I think that's the most typical example of Japanese gay guys who live in Tokyo. I would suggest that almost all Japanese guys in *Ni-chome* only have friends who come from there. In their formative years, they've been exposed to that kind of culture."

Sean didn't meet his boyfriend's family for a long time.

"While we were living together, he began to have some form of relationship with my mother. I told her all about him and she'd been interested in knowing him. Eventually, they met. I have a pretty small family. They don't live in London, but we had a small holiday in London. He also met my friends. I wanted to see how he would cope with that. Would he really get along with all these people? Would living in the UK be OK? He was totally fine.

"But his family was completely in the dark. I hadn't met any of his family before I got married. His family knew he was living with a foreigner, but they just assumed that we were roommates. Now his family know he is gay, but his father didn't know it until after we moved in together.

"Even when we rented an apartment, the people we rented it from didn't know. It was all kind of pretend conversation. When we went to the real estate agency, they said, 'OK, two guys living together, obviously you need a 2LDK (a two-bedroom apartment).' I said yes and pretended to be co-habiting together. He needed a guarantor and I needed one too."

"How did his family take the fact that you guys are together?"

"Actually, pretty well. I thought they would take it very badly because it had been a secret. Basically, it was a lie because he had told them something different. But in the end, they were very positive about it."

"How did you decide to come back to London?"

"It was mainly my decision. A few things happened at the same time. I was kind of bored with my work. I was working for quite a small company, although the customers were quite good and the salary was fine. I'd gone from being a teacher to being a behind-the-scenes manager. Our company had been recovering from the financial crisis but then the big earthquake happened. And there was another big problem with selling products to clients.

"Actually, he didn't really enjoy living in Tokyo. So when I said to him, 'Let's get married and leave,' he really wanted to do that."

"How did you propose?"

"It wasn't actually romantic. I woke up and he was in the other room. We had a minor falling out. He wasn't angry but just a little bit cranky.

"The one slightly romantic aspect was that it was the same day Prince William and Kate Middleton got married. The plan was to invite all the foreigners who came from the Commonwealth countries to my friend's house to watch the royal wedding, and to propose in front of everybody just before the wedding started. But because we had this slight argument, he was in a bad mood and I thought he was not going to the party. So I just kind of said it over breakfast.

"It totally caught him off guard and he said, 'Ah, yes.' So we spend the morning looking for an engagement ring."

"What do you like about your husband?"

"He's a somewhat calm and level-headed person, although he can be a little bit self-centered. For me that's not a problem at all. Some Japanese guys get taken care of by their mothers and then their wives. There's an element of it. For example, I'm a lot handier around the house because I prefer to have things done in a certain way. He's happy to let that slide on his part, because he knows I'm going to do it. Judging by the place he used to live in, I can see that. Mostly, other people who lived in the apartment cleaned it up.

"He's artistic, creative, and also adventurous. I'm willing to take a risk because I'm not risk averse. Most Japanese people are hugely risk averse, but he's not like that. In that respect, he's slightly un-Japanese, which is not necessarily why I'm attracted to him, but it makes things easier.

"It was a year and a half later that we finally left and came here to London. We had to start applying for the visa six months before we left. The visa process was actually smooth. I used to work for a government agency here in London, so I'm very familiar with how you write the application form. So many people who apply for passports and visas make huge mistakes. But I knew exactly what to write so I wrote it myself without using a lawyer.

"Here, the relationship is much easier. I've always found that relationships in Japan are quite stressful because of the environment and the number of obligations you have to fulfill. Here, we don't really have awkward social interactions. It's totally fine for him to say, 'I'm meeting these people for dinner. Do you want to come?' and I say no. And he knows he can do the same thing. If I was in Japan and did the same thing, other people would say, 'Where is he?' because it would be odd to be seen by yourself.

"Here, my landlord who lives next door knows everything about us. The people I work with know everything about me and what my situation is. In Japan, I'd always have to take off my wedding ring. I didn't mind telling people about my situation, but as soon as they saw the ring they would ask, 'Did you marry a Japanese woman?' and I had to correct them. It would become awkward, which people didn't like, so I'd always have to cover up.

"I hope I didn't paint too much of the negative sides of Japan. I don't have any regret at all about my time in Japan. People I've known in Japan are happy in their lives these days even though things may have been tough at the time."

Discussions

In Japan, LGBT people are not always visible in public. *Ni-chome* is one of the few places where gay people openly hold each other and kiss on the street. But elsewhere, you hardly recognize gay people because they don't necessarily dress "gay" or show affection in public. Also, as of 2014, same-sex marriage is not recognized in Japan or in other Asian countries.

Some people remark that Japanese people simply don't talk about LGBT people in general. For example, a lot of Japanese celebrities don't come out, let alone speak vocally about their sexuality. I've never observed hostility towards LGBT people in Japan, but this doesn't mean LGBT rights are widely recognized.

Another interesting element of Sean's stories is how guys in *Ni-chome* are different from guys elsewhere. This is somewhat related to how people in Roppongi tend to be different from the ones who don't go there. In Japan, there seem to be a lot of small communities of like-minded people. Each community has its own particular atmosphere and people in these communities—whether they are hobby groups or particular venues—can express values that the average Japanese person doesn't necessarily share. I think *Ni-chome* is a good example of that.

11. Natasha—Why aren't Japanese guys interested in sex?

A Russian girl's bittersweet experience with Japanese guys

W HEN THE SOVIET UNION WAS falling apart, a Japanese tourist visited Saint Petersburg, a beautiful city known for white nights when the sun never fully goes down. It was his first time in the Soviet Union.

There, he met a beautiful Russian woman. She was his tour guide. She had studied Japanese in university and had always been interested in Japan. It didn't take long for him to fall in love with her. During the trip, he proposed to her.

"Come back to Japan with me," he said.

"I'm sorry. I can't. I'm pregnant," she said.

He didn't insist. "But we could stay friends," he said. They exchanged addresses and he went back to Japan.

He started supporting her. The Soviet people were having a hard time and there was no food. He would buy her husband's paintings so she would have enough money for her family.

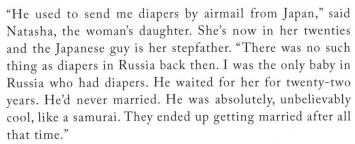

"He used to send me diapers by airmail from Japan," said Natasha, the woman's daughter. She's now in her twenties and the Japanese guy is her stepfather. "There was no such thing as diapers in Russia back then. I was the only baby in Russia who had diapers. He waited for her for twenty-two years. He'd never married. He was absolutely, unbelievably cool, like a samurai. They ended up getting married after all that time."

Her mother moved to Japan when Natasha was little. Since then, she would come to Japan once in a while to meet her mother.

The classmate

Natasha grew up with strict grandparents. They didn't allow her to spend much time outside the school. She didn't have many friends. She stayed inside, reading books and studying.

"Surprisingly, when I was fifteen, while my grandparents were keeping an eye on me, I managed to get a boyfriend. I was going to a private school and the classes were really small. There were only five people in my class: four girls and one boy. That particular boy became my boyfriend.

"It was a Valentine's Day's party. I convinced my grandparents to let me go and stay out late. We went to this café. There were people from school there. Eventually, everybody left and there was only him and me.

"I didn't actually expect anything to happen. We were just talking and talking and suddenly kissing. It was a very mutual thing.

"I have very fond memories of that relationship. We used to skip school, and that was the only time we could spend time together. There was no going out at night because it wasn't allowed. My city was very beautiful, so we just walked around. There were a lot of interesting places like science museums where you could touch stuff and see how it worked. There was a planetarium and a cinema. Or we could just sit in a café for hours."

"Did you guys have any conflicts?"

"Sometimes. There was a girl in our class and we fought about her a lot. She was really, really pretty. I still consider her one of the most beautiful women I've ever met. We were all good friends. In Russia, it's very common to be very close to your friends. You can kiss on the cheek and no one's going to think it's weird. He and she used to go out together. I'm pretty sure nothing really happened, but I was still kind of jealous. They would always ask me if it was OK if they went out together. She was allowed to go out all the time. So I was the one who was stuck at home.

"When we fought, it always started with talking and it escalated. He was a very emotional person and I was too. I remember him breaking his phone. He used to break stuff and I was always angry. I was like, 'You're damaging valuable things just because you're angry. It's so ridiculous.' Now, looking back, it was kind of funny.

"When I came to Japan, it became a long-distance relationship. We tried our best to work it out, but I decided to stay. So we decided it wasn't working. It was, of course, very hard. But we are still friends. I guess that first experience was the template for my later relationships. And I was lucky to have that."

The home party guy

Natasha came to Japan to go to university partly because she didn't think going to Russian universities was a good option, and partly because she would be able to live with her mother for the first time. She came to Hokkaido, a northern island of the size of Ireland.

First, she went to a language school to study Japanese.

"I dated two guys. The first one was a Russian guy I met in a club. He was eleven years older than me. Then I actually managed to get a Japanese boyfriend. I was starting to understand the language and I figured that if you got close to a Japanese person, it was useful.

"I met him at a home party. A mutual friend introduced us. He was twenty-five. He spoke English, maybe because he used to travel a lot. But his English wasn't entirely perfect. It was just good enough to communicate. It was a party with a group of Japanese people who hang out with foreigners. He liked going to those kinds of gatherings.

"On our first date, we went driving, and then we went to this bar in a fancy hotel on the top floor. But it was just that. After the first date, we went on a second date. And then, you know, when you say 'I like you' in Japanese, it means..."

"A *kokuhaku* (confession of love)?"

"Yeah, that was *kokuhaku*. But in my head 'I like you' in Japanese just meant 'I like you and maybe I want to go out with you.' I didn't realize it was serious, so he had to explain that he'd actually done the *kokuhaku* thing. I didn't know anything about Japanese culture then.

"He would take me out. He would say, 'Let's go driving.' In Hokkaido, there were a lot of mountains so the night view was very nice. And there were so many nice restaurants! The food was unbelievable. I miss it so much. He used to take me to these small restaurants. I think he was quite rich, so he could afford a fancy, big BMW. I don't think he went to university. But he was from a wealthy family.

"The relationship didn't last long. He used to take me out a lot and show me off. Not in a bad way, of course. There were a lot of home parties in Hokkaido because there weren't many places to go to and everybody's house was big. He always insisted that I come with him.

"I think he really enjoyed being with me. I used to ask a lot of questions about Japan. 'Why's everybody so polite?' or that sort of thing. He told me about his high school sports club. He was on a baseball team. We don't have that in Russia, so it was interesting. In Japan, they put so much effort into physical education. It's almost like an army. It's crazy.

"But he was very possessive. It the beginning, he was very nice and charming. But he texted me all the time. 'What are you doing?' 'What are you eating?' 'Who are you with?'

"And he gave me stuff. Nothing too expensive, but he would ask me 'Where did you put that bear?' If he gave me a phone strap and I didn't have it on my phone, he would ask me where it was. That gradually became annoying, and that's why I broke up with him.

"I remember going out with my mom and her friends. There was this guy with his wife and son. I used to hang out with them a lot when I was a child, because they were always in Hokkaido. My boyfriend was also there with his friends. When he saw us, he went completely crazy. He said, 'You are with a man!' The man was forty years old, but he didn't care.

"We had a fight. We did get back together after, but I wasn't comfortable with him anymore. We still saw each other, but less and less. The moment I stopped answering those hundreds of emails a day, he somehow lost interest.

"There's this very famous Russian poet, Pushkin, who wrote something like, 'The more you love a woman, the less she loves you.' That was exactly what happened."

The math teacher

After two years of language school, she moved to Yokohama, a city of 3.7 million near Tokyo. She did another two years of language school because her first school didn't qualify as official education.

"There, she met another Japanese guy.

"He was helping me out with math. I had to take the entrance exam and my math was—and still is—horrible. I didn't even know what differential calculus was because I didn't do that in high school in Russia. So my friend introduced me to this guy from Waseda University. He was so nice and caring. He spent hours and hours explaining to me the stuff I couldn't understand. He would buy me drinks and ask me if I ate enough.

"Occasionally, after a lesson, we would go for a walk in the city. Even when it was really late, I would go out because I lived around there and didn't have to worry about the last train.

"That particular evening, we walked a lot. Yokohama has a lot of romantic cafés and restaurants, and the view is also very nice. It was summer and it was warm. We stayed out all night until the morning. We walked and walked and sat down somewhere and had coffee. Then we kissed. I didn't see it coming, because he was very shy. He was twenty-six or twenty-seven back then. I was just turning twenty-one.

"We stayed together for a while, but then he left to go to Switzerland on a scholarship. He was getting a Ph.D. in math. But after he left, we kept calling and emailing each other. He came back to Japan once, and we were still together.

"It was an extremely calm relationship. It was nice, but I think I got bored. I remember we broke up over email. I had to write a really long message. He said, 'It's very sad, but it's OK.'

"He's married now. I was at his wedding two months ago. He found a half-Japanese and half-Swiss girl from Switzerland. They met exactly two years ago, so I think it was after I broke up with him. I don't think he would have had the strength to maintain two relationships at the same time. The girl is very quiet and calm as well. It was obvious that I wasn't perfect for him, but I felt lonely and he was a very comfortable guy.

"But he was surprisingly good at kissing for a shy guy. He was a very educated person, so it was easy to talk to him. I don't think the first Japanese guy went to university at all because I couldn't talk to him about serious stuff like culture, music, films, books, or anything. I consider myself an educated person and I like to talk about philosophy, such as the views of Emmanuel Kant. When I met the second Russian guy, we were in a club discussing Dostoevsky."

"Do you see any differences between Russian and Japanese guys?"

"So that thing, *kokuhaku*, only happened to me once. But the idea of saying that you like the person before you do anything is very strange to me. How can you possibly like a person if you haven't spent any time with them? How could you possibly know that you are physically compatible?

"The second guy did it like European guys. He just went for it. He told me he loved me after weeks.

"The Russian guy I met after, he said he loved me really fast. But we'd known each other for a long time. I knew I loved him, but I was really scared to say it. I remember telling him, 'I'm not ready yet.' I didn't say it until almost the very last month, because in my opinion, it was a very serious thing to say."

The German guy

"I was sitting in a café in Marunouchi (Tokyo's main business area). I was writing a paper for my university on my computer. A guy was sitting behind me. He saw me writing in Japanese and he was impressed. I left the place and went to the station. He followed me and talked to me on the street. I never answer people on the street, but for some reason I did that day. After that, we started spending some time together. We went to the café again. We went running together. He took me out to places in Roppongi. We stayed friends for a while and then it just happened.

"He took me to Thailand on winter break. It was so cold and horrible in Tokyo because it was January. He just sent me the tickets by email and said, 'Be at the airport.' It was amazing and I've loved Thailand since then.

"I still have all those good memories. It just wasn't meant to work out. His father was very ill and so he had to go back to Germany.

"He also had two daughters, and they were entering their teenage stage and having some trouble. He was divorced. And I totally understood. He had to be there for them. He did the opposite of what my father did and rightly so. His daughters are much more important than any girl you meet in Marunouchi.

"We were together for a year and broke up just a month ago. I'm still not completely over him. He has everything I like in a person. He's very intelligent. He's funny. He doesn't look his age, but he's experienced. It's very flattering that a person who is that old and experienced is still interested in me. I like that feeling.

"I keep trying to prove to myself that I'm still interesting to older people. I guess it's very cliché because I didn't have a father in my life. The math teacher was much older too. After I broke up with the German guy, I met a Norwegian guy. He is thirty and very handsome. He's very romantic and gentle, but quite young by my standards. He hit on me, but I said, 'Sorry I can't.' And he was very sad about it.

"I keep getting into relationships with people who unable to physically be with me. I have to stop dating expats and people who are not going to be in Japan forever. I'm probably not going to stay in Japan myself."

Sex in Japan

"I've dated people from a lot of different countries. People can be different, so I can't say Japanese people are all like this and that. But based on my experience, Japanese people are not very good in bed.

"I've dated two Japanese guys, and of course we had sex. I'm really sorry to say this, but neither of them was good in bed. Maybe I'm comparing them to Germans, which might not be fair. Size doesn't really matter, but technique does. I'm a very active person in bed, but when I started to move and tried to do something, the Japanese guys kind of freaked out. They were like, 'What are you doing? Get back!'

"I guess most girls are passive in bed. It's the main complaint guys always have. In Russia, we say that when a girl like that gets into bed, she turns into a piece of wood. I'm not a piece of wood. Well, Japanese guys can't be a hundred percent passive, because they have to do something. So there is something, but it's not enough! I also like it when a man is rough with me. Nothing too scary. I just wouldn't mind pulling on the hair or something. But they don't do it even if I ask. They are like, 'Oh my God, I can't do that.' That's the most unsatisfactory part.

"That's what puzzles me about Japan. There is this *shibari* (Japanese-style rope bondage art) thing. And there's also *shunga* (traditional Japanese pornographic visual art). But there's this really conservative and passive actual thing. I really don't understand. *Shibari* is beautiful. I actually saw a show once, back in Hokkaido. There was this couple. He was a professional and she was a model. You could see how their feelings were translated into this action. It was very passionate and very arousing too.

"My first relationship with the Russian guy was very long. That was where I got all these experiences. But there's so much more to try. Japanese guys are kind of scared when you ask them to spank you. That's really weird. It's ultimately wrong. There has to be more.

"I have this friend who's a dancer in a club. She used to work in a soap land (Japanese brothel) in Yoshiwara because she was in a difficult situation. She talks about sex openly. She always says the same thing. 'Why aren't Japanese guys interested in sex?' She's a very passionate woman. She talks about it very graphically. She talks about how the process was and how big the guy was. She had this boyfriend. They'd been seeing each other for a year and only had sex five times. Five times! It's not even once a month. It's not even once in two months. That's crazy.

"And then there are these really innocent twenty-one-year-old girls from university. They are sometimes still virgins and don't know what all the fuss is about. I have this Korean friend who just turned thirty. She's never, ever had a boyfriend in her life. She's a lovely person, but I think she's very picky. She keeps expecting the perfect guy who is nowhere to be found.

"We had a mutual friend who was interested in her. He invited her to his place to 'watch a movie,' which basically didn't really mean just 'watch a movie.' But she was sure he actually wanted to watch a movie. She went to his place and there was no one else, and there was a television, but it wasn't on. She thought it was weird, but she stayed. He started touching her. She ran away. She was absolutely not expecting it. I keep telling her that she needs to find someone because it's getting ridiculous.

"I remember going out with the math teacher. He always wanted to hold my hand. But I always wanted to hug him. He would run away from a hug. He would say, 'Don't. It's uncomfortable to walk like that.' It is uncomfortable to walk, but that's not the point.

"And then there is a sex department store in Akihabara. It has seven floors. I went there with the German guy. We were buying condoms. There were many Japanese condoms, but I really didn't know what to choose. So I asked a guy in the shop for recommendations holding two boxes of condoms. I was like, 'Which one is better?'" The guy totally freaked out! His jaw dropped. He worked in a sex shop, but he wasn't expecting questions from customers. But maybe he was confused because we were a foreign couple asking explicit questions in Japanese."

Friendzoned

"I have so many male friends who tried to get into a relationship with me. Mostly Japanese, actually. We spent time together all the time because we were close friends. We were not out on dates. I never let them pay for things. I even went traveling with one of them because I really wanted to go. I made it absolutely clear that I was with someone else at that time, but he still tried to hold my hand.

"There was one other guy I hung out with for a while, and then he invited me to a bar at the Park Hyatt in Shinjuku. You know, the super expensive bar in *Lost in Translation*. He suddenly said, 'I love you.' I wasn't expecting it. We had been friends for almost a year. I said, 'Sorry, I can't. I'm with someone else.' Then he was very angry. He said, 'I paid for this whole thing.'

"It was easy for me to become friends with guys—easier than with girls. But they always ended up falling in love with me. It's sad for me, because the moment I say 'no,' it's over. They stop texting, calling, or seeing you, as if the friendship was never there. I can think of four guys who were like that.

"Maybe I get too close, because, as you say, Japanese people are not really physically affectionate. I'm not intentionally leading them on. But the thing is, if those guys had pushed earlier, we might actually have had something. If I spend too much time with a man when I'm not with him, it means I'm not going to be with him ever."

Discussions

When Natasha's first boyfriend said he liked her, she didn't understand what he really meant. His intention was to ask her to be his girlfriend. This is what we call *kokuhaku* (confession of love) and it is a very important concept in Japanese dating.

Another interesting observation is that her two Japanese boyfriends were not very passionate in bed. I have the same impression about Japanese girls. This may also be cultural because Japanese people are usually not emotionally expressive and physically affectionate. It is possible that a small amount of stimulation is enough for the average Japanese.

Natasha also talks about her male friends who turned out to be interested in her. They are so-called "nice guys" who approach girls under the pretense of making friends while hiding their romantic interests. Their mistake, of course, is not being upfront about their true intentions. This is the opposite of what Charles, the British guy, did. He didn't hide his feelings for the Japanese girl even though she wasn't interested in him initially. Eventually, she said yes and he ended up marrying her.

12. Andre—When she came back, she was a different person

Marriages, broken relationships, and lost girlfriends of an ex-Marine

Andre looks young. One of the most shocking moments in my life was when I learned how old he was. I had known him for a couple of years, but it had never occurred to me that he was actually forty-two. Come to think of it, his experience was just too rich for him to be in his thirties.

He was born and raised in Jamaica until he turned eleven. Then he moved to New York and got American citizenship. He joined the US Marines after high school and came to Japan for the first time.

"Did you date anybody before you came to Japan?" I asked.

"Yeah, of course," he said. "I left my high school girlfriend back in New York. We kept in touch. We sent letters back and forth until it kind of fizzled off. She was born in America, but she wasn't really from America. She was of Southeast

Asian descent. I've always had a favorite 'type' so to speak. She had long, straight, black hair. Her skin was almost like chocolate, or more like a caramel complexion, like Japanese girls who have tans."

The girl at the gate

"My first true Asian girlfriend was from Okinawa. This was three months after I got here. I was nineteen.

"One day, I was going off base, as I sometimes did. I usually just walked because I didn't have a car. At the base entrance, there was a checking gate which you could enter only if you were military personnel or if you were with military personnel. That day, there was a Japanese girl standing there. She was looking outside, not inside. I looked at her, but I passed by.

"I was out walking around, having something to eat, and going to a bar for drinks. This probably went on for about three or four hours. The sun was going down. It was dark. I came back, and she was still standing there. At first I passed by again, but then I thought, *huh, let's go back. Maybe she's waiting for somebody in a barrack*. So I went back and asked her if she was waiting for someone. She said, 'Yeah my boyfriend was supposed to meet me here.' I said, 'Which barrack does he live in?' It was pretty far away from where I stayed and I didn't know who he was. So I said, 'OK, good luck then.'

"A couple days later, I went off base again. And there she was, standing there. I stopped and I talked to her for a while. He had never showed up the last time. She had no idea if he'd left Japan or if he was going on another deployment. We had monthly deployments. We would go on a boat to the other islands, like the Philippines or Korea.

"I told her, 'Things can happen. If you haven't heard from him within a few days, it's up to you if you want to wait or not.' Then I left. When I came back, she wasn't there. I thought either she had found him or had decided to leave.

"About a week later, I was doing the same routine trip off base again. She was standing there. I said, 'Wow, are you still waiting for this guy?' She said, 'No, actually, I'm waiting for you.' 'Why?' 'Well, of all the people that walked by me here, no one stopped to ask except you. You seem like a nice guy. I'd like to talk to you.' So we talked. She came with me on my off base trip and we had a drink. She said she had been dating this guy for about six months, but no one really knew what had happened. We hung out for a couple of weeks after that, and we decided to start dating.

"When I finished work, I would meet her at the gate. We went out to town, and went to bars or watched a movie. People were allowed to come on base in the daytime, so I would invite her on weekends. It was fun. It was good to have someone.

"After a while, we met some of her friends and one took a liking to me. We talked and talked. My girlfriend started getting jealous. I told her there was nothing going on. The girl did like me, but our interaction was also a way for her to practice English.

"They were different. My girlfriend at the time had just finished school and wanted to go out and have fun. The other girl was a little older. She had finished school and was helping her parents in Naha (the capital of Okinawa). They owned a store and we were always going there. It was fun. It was nice to hang out with more than one girl. Even though you have a girlfriend, as long as you are faithful, then it's fine to hang out with other girls. But, at the time in Okinawa, the reputation the military guys had wasn't good, so my girlfriend didn't trust me.

"After a while, our relationship kind of fizzled out. It didn't go where I thought it would. But again, I found her at the gate! A short time after that, I started dating the other girl seriously. I was already close to her. Unlike the first one who liked to go out and party, the other one liked to relax and walk around. She was calm."

The Haitian girl

After Okinawa, he went back to the States and spent a couple of decades there.

"I left Okinawa and the second girlfriend behind. I had to go to college. One of the reasons I joined the military was to pay for college. I went to school and got a part-time job. It wasn't easy. It took me a good six to eight years to finish my first degree, and another three years to finish my second. I never went back to Okinawa. I lost touch with the second girl.

"Back in New York, I dated a Spanish girl. I wasn't dating for a long-term thing anymore. I was just dating for fun. When the fun ended, the relationship ended. After the Spanish girl, I dated a Haitian girl who was working with me. That actually lasted six years.

"She was born in Haiti and had immigrated to the US just like I did. I was working for a movie theater, and that was where I met her. We wanted to move to Texas, so I spoke to my boss and asked for a transfer to Texas. I moved to Texas and she was supposed to come down later, but she got sick. She had cancer. I packed up and moved back to New York. A few months later, she passed away. We were actually engaged."

The chat room girl

"After my fiancée passed away, I dated a white girl for three months. She was Hungarian, and I think what she wanted was a visa. She always talked about getting married. She'd say, 'It doesn't have to be serious. I just want to get married.' I said, 'Yeah, if I got married, it would not be because someone wants a visa. It would be because I love someone.'

"But then, eventually, I ended up marrying a Japanese girl in the States and part of the reason was that I wanted to go to Japan. She wanted to come to the States too, and this was the easiest way.

"I went on the Internet looking for chat rooms for Japanese people in New York. I met Japanese girls. I came to Japan in 2004 and went to Tokyo to see them. I was in Japan for only a month, but I wanted to come back here the very next year.

"A few days before I was about to go back to the States, I spoke to one of the girls. She wanted to go to the States. So I said, 'Why don't we get married?' She said, 'Really?' I said, 'You like me and I like you, so why not?' So we decided to get married. We went to city hall in Japan and signed the document. Then I went back to the States and filled out the necessary documents.

"She moved to the States. It was new and interesting. I still had to go to work and school. For the first part of the six months or so, she did nothing. She was just hanging around. Then after the paperwork was done, she decided to get a job. We moved back to Connecticut because of my job. She traveled from there on the train down to New York to go to work. We didn't spend a lot of time together.

"Time passed, and the more time we spent together, the more we realized we had nothing in common. She wanted to stay in the States, but I wanted to go to Japan. But she didn't want to come back to Japan. I said, 'OK, you got what you wanted, but I got screwed over with what I wanted. I'm out.'

"I don't think I ever loved her, even at the beginning. I was mostly infatuated with the fact that she was Japanese because there weren't many Japanese people in the States. I thought I could show her off to my friends. I don't think she loved me either. She told me she did, but I don't think she did. She liked me because I was black. She was one of those types—she liked black men."

The jealous girl

Andre came to Japan again in 2010.

"I like familiarity. If I am with someone for more than six months, then I'm familiar with that person. I tell girls, 'I'm going to be somewhat of a stranger for the first six months. I'm getting to know you and trying to see what you are like. If you survive six months of being with me and going places with me, I can call you my 'girlfriend.'

"I met a girl at my friend's party. At the time, I didn't have a girlfriend and I wasn't really looking for one. She didn't have a boyfriend and according to her, she wasn't looking for one either. But we hung out so often that we just ended up being together.

"I realized that when Japanese girls tell you they are not looking for a relationship, it means they are. They say, 'Yeah I'm not really looking for a relationship. So do you want to hang out?' And then they are like, 'Can I be your girlfriend?' It was just like that the third time.

"With her, I was thinking, 'OK, I like her and she seems fun. Let's hang out and see what happens.' But after the fourth or fifth time, she asked, 'So, what am I?' I said, 'What do you mean? You are my friend.' She asked, 'Is that it?' I was thinking, *OK, we have slept together but does that automatically make her my girlfriend?* So I told her, 'Six months. You have to get past six months. If you can survive the first six months, then, possibly I can move you from a friend or friends with benefits camp to the girlfriend camp.'

"When I was nineteen, I learned that if someone holds my hand, my body temperature goes up. So the moment someone puts their hand in mine, it starts to sweat. I don't like that. I kept trying to explain this to her. But holding hands was one of the things that she always wanted to do. We'd be sitting down at a table and she wanted to reach out and hold my hand across the table. I would think, 'We're sitting. We're looking at each other. Why do I need to be reaching across the table?' She just never got it. I tried to talk to her about that, and she'd say, 'OK, OK.' But after half an hour you could see that she would fidget. She had a need to be touched.

"We went to a bar in Shibuya where I did most of my events. She came there to perform because she was a dancer. I had my painting performance there too. I had to switch between MC and painting, which meant I didn't have time for anything else. By the time I was finished at the end of the night, she was jealous. So she decided to get involved in my painting performance as well. That was her way of getting all the attention.

"And then, the same question came up: 'What am I?' I said, 'We had this conversation before. What do you mean "What are you?"' She let it go for another week. Then another week came around and she said, 'My friends want to know if I have a boyfriend. What should I tell them?' It went on like that for the next two or three months.

"Six months went by and I'd had enough. I couldn't deal with her anymore. I said, 'I can't say that you're my girlfriend. Honestly, I just see another problem developing out of this. You are nagging me to be my girlfriend. But if I say you're my girlfriend, what's the next thing you're going to say? When are we getting engaged? Getting married? Having kids? I'm not ready for any of that.'

"We broke up, got back together, broke up, got back together, and broke up again. In the end, we went our separate ways."

The single mother

"After that experience, I met another girl at one of my friend's parties. I was sitting in the back by myself because I had sprained my ankle. She and a bunch of her friends came over. They sat down next to me, and decided to drag me off to the floor and make me dance. But my ankle was not so good. Apparently, she had a boyfriend at the time. So we just exchanged contact numbers.

"That coming weekend, there was a pizza and beer thing at my usual bar. I invited her and all of the other people. She sent me a message back saying she couldn't make it because the day after that, she had a dance thing in Tokyo. She asked me if I wanted to come.

"At the event, I watched her dance and it was fun. Then I didn't talk to her for a while. From time to time, she would send me a message saying, 'Hey, how are you doing? We should hang out.' I'd say, 'Oh, sure. Just let me know when.' And then I would hear nothing again. Maybe a couple of months later, she again wrote, 'Hey we should hang out!' I said, 'Sure, let me know when.' And then nothing.

"I posted a picture of a sunset on my Facebook wall. She commented on it and we started to chat. She asked, 'Why haven't we hung out yet?' I said, 'Well, you keep saying we should. You don't tell me when.' So she said, 'Oh, OK. So how about this day and that day?' So we finally met and hung out. That day, we talked about things we liked and didn't like. But apparently, she would forget everything I said later on.

"We started dating, but she was in a rush for everything. She was a few years older than me. At the time, I thought I was ready to settle. I thought, *this may actually work out, she might be the one.*

"I went through the usual process. She asked, 'So, what am I?' I said, 'You're my friend.' She said, 'That's it?' I said, 'Obviously I'm more than a friend to you, but it's only been a month. What do you want?' I told her my process. But she said, 'Oh, if you don't introduce me as your girlfriend, then we are finished.' So I went to my usual bar and did something I would never do. The people there are like my family. If I bring someone there and introduce them as my girlfriend, it means I'm serious. That time, I took her and I actually introduced her to everyone as my girlfriend.

"After that, everything kind of started spiraling downward.

"I was on the phone with her and she said, 'What are you going to do tonight?' I said, 'I was supposed to go to the usual bar, but I don't really feel like it, so I might not go.' She said, 'OK, I've got some stuff to do, so let's chat later.' After that, I was home alone and bored. I thought, 'Well, what the hell. It's just a short walk to the bar.' So I decided to go.

"She called me later and said, 'Where are you?'

'Actually, I'm on my way to the bar.'

'I thought you weren't going.'

'I thought I wasn't going too, but I changed my mind.'

'Why did you change your mind?'

'You weren't on the phone with me when I changed my mind, so I didn't tell you.'

"Why was I having that conversation? I was not allowed to change my mind?

"Another time, I took a picture with my friend at the bar because my friend asked me to. I posted the picture on Facebook. Then I got a text from her, 'You don't even care how I feel!' I said, 'Huh? What do you mean?' She said,

'Nothing,' and she stopped texting. I texted her and then tried to call her. But she didn't pick up the phone.

"I sent a message, 'I don't know what's going on, but I'm coming over. Let's talk.' She didn't reply. When you use Line (a popular messaging app in Japan), you can see when someone has read your message, so I knew that she knew I was coming over. If she didn't want me to come, all she had to do was say, 'Don't.' No reply, so I took it as a yes. She liked flowers and plants so when I got off at the station, I bought a rose and a houseplant.

"I went to her house, rang the bell, and she came to the door and opened it. I presented the flower. She smiled and gave me a hug. She was jealous because my friend had used my phone to take a picture. She said, 'Why can't they use their phones?' Is it a cultural thing? Because people take pictures with my phone all the time. Before I met her, I took pictures of all the people around me all the time. I'm actually a photographer. That's what I do. Have you seen how many albums I have on my Facebook?

"But I said 'OK, fine' because I didn't want to fight and make this bigger than it was. That situation diffused, and we spent the night together. I got up the next morning and went home.

"Everything seemed OK. I planned a trip to go to Okinawa. I hadn't been to Okinawa for years, and she wanted to go too. Before the trip, I had to go back to New York for Thanksgiving in November. When I was in New York, I stayed connected with her. We chatted on Line, and sometimes I called her from my phone. Everything seemed good.

"I came back from New York and we went to Okinawa. We went to an aquarium, a zoo, a castle, an old temple, another island... we had a good time.

"One evening, we went to visit my old military base. We drove to the base, but couldn't get in because I didn't have the pass anymore. I just spoke to one of guys at the gate. After that, we looked for something to eat. It started to rain.

"The first day in Okinawa, I had chosen what I wanted to eat: seafood. So that night, I asked her to choose. I said, 'I can't eat pork, but you can. You can choose a place.' But she couldn't decide what to eat. We drove for a good half an hour. It was raining and she still couldn't decide. So I was like, 'OK, fine. There's a *yakiniku* place.' At *yakiniku* they have usually more than one kind of meat. She didn't have any objections at the time. She picked what she wanted, and I picked mostly chicken and vegetables.

"We got back to Tokyo on Monday. I had to work in the afternoon so I had to go straight to work directly from the airport. I knew I had to do that, so I had brought my stuff for work along with me. I thought things were good. It was the end of December.

"She had a son. She had been married and divorced. In fact, her son doesn't know his father. Her son was in the States and went to school there, but he was coming back mid-December so I didn't see her for a week. On December 27th, she and her son went to Egypt. I didn't go. I didn't ask and she didn't offer. I met her on the 26th before she left. It was the day after Christmas. I got her a tripod and a remote so she could take pictures in Egypt. In Okinawa, we always wanted to take pictures of us together, but we always had to find some place to put the camera or ask somebody to do it. It was a Christmas present.

"When she came back, she was a different person. I swear the person who came back wasn't the person who left. The day she came back, I was at work. She was on the train, going from the airport to her house. She texted me, 'I'm back and I'm on the train going home. Let's have lunch.' I was at work, so there was no way I could have had lunch with her. So I told her. No reply. None whatsoever. I thought, 'OK, she's tired, so she went home.'

"That night, when I got home, I texted, 'Hey, how was your trip?' I got 'read' on Line. No reply. I went to bed, got up the next day and texted, 'Hey, how are you?' No reply. I had a Japanese class. I went to the class and finished it. Still nothing.

"Two days later, it was a Sunday. Still no reply. I figured she was busy with her son. He was going back to the States in a couple of days. So I decided not to message her.

"Then her son left. Still no reply. However, I'd seen pictures she put on Facebook from some events she went to. I sent her a message asking, 'Hey, what's going on?' Her reply was, 'Could you leave me alone for a while?' I said, 'Is everything OK?' She said, 'Damn it. Don't you know when to shut up?' I was like, 'OK. I'm shutting up.'

"It went on like that for almost two weeks. Then I got a 'Hi' from her. What the fuck? But I said, 'Hi, how are you?'

'I'm coming home from work.'

'What you are cooking?'

'Some kind of fish.'

'Sounds good. I'd love to have some.'

'Really? You don't eat fish.'

'What?'

'You told me you didn't like fish.'

'No! I don't like octopus. I don't like squid. I don't like eel. But that's pretty much all the fish I don't like. In fact, when we went to Okinawa, we were at the seafood restaurant the first night, remember? It was my choice. Are you OK?'

The response to that was, 'Yeah, I'm fine.'

"Sometimes, you can feel the emotions coming through the text. I said, 'You say you're OK. But you're not. I'd like to see you.' She said, 'I'm busy.'

"The next week, Friday night, I wasn't feeling too well, so I stayed home. Monday morning, I decided to go to the doctor before going to work. I talked to her over the phone on the way to the doctor. The entire time, not once did she ever say, 'I want to see you.'

"The doctor told me I had the flu and that I had to stay away from people for five days. I sent her a text, 'Guess what...' Her response to that was, 'Oh no. I was going to tell you to meet me for dinner tonight.' What? Why didn't you tell me that before? If you had told me before I went to the doctor, it would've actually meant more.

"When I got better, I texted her, 'Hey, I'm better.' I was usually the one who would say, 'Hey, do you want to meet?' But this time, I decided to let her suggest that we meet. I texted, 'Yeah, I'm better. I can go out again. I can see people,' and waited to see if she took the hint.

"Three days went by. Still nothing. Very limited chat. I thought, *enough is enough. What the hell is going on?* I said, 'We are not kids. This is not school. We are not playing games. This was what you pushed for. You wanted to have a boyfriend. What the fuck?' She said, 'We should talk. Come to my place.'

"That day, the entire day, it was texts as usual. In the morning, she sent me a message, 'Hey, how are you doing?' and throughout the day, we were chatting back and forth. Halfway through the day, the chat changed from just regular banter to complaints. The complaints were about everything I had done wrong since the first day.

"She never ever gave me a straight reason why she wanted to break up. It was something like, 'You don't like pork.' I can't eat pork, but actually I love it. I just can't eat it. She said, 'I went to Okinawa. I wanted pork because Okinawa is famous for pork, but I couldn't eat it because of you.'

'Why because of me? I told you to eat it.'

'Yeah, but if you can't eat it, I can't eat it.'

'You can eat it! I don't have to eat what you eat.'

She also said, 'You told me you didn't like raw fish.'

'When? Sushi is one of the things I like.'

'You like sweet things and I don't.'

'Fine, so when we go out and have dessert, I'll eat your dessert. You don't have to eat it.'

"Another episode happened when we had gone to see the illumination (a holiday light display) at Sagami Lake. We went there in December before we went to Okinawa. They had this ropeway that went up to the top of the hill. It was night and it was freaking freezing. We had already walked around and taken a bunch of pictures. There was this huge, long line. We stood in the line for five minutes, freezing. She got a hot coffee from one of the vending machines and I put my hands around it to keep them warm. I said to her, 'Do you want to leave?' She said, 'I want to see the stuff up there, but it's cold. I'll wait with you if you want to wait. But if you want to leave, let's leave.' So I said, 'Let's leave.'

"Apparently, in that exchange, I missed her real intent. Her real intent was to stay there in the cold and go up the hill.

"I never treated her badly or unkindly. If anything, I treated her too kindly. Maybe I was too nice. Because, honestly, to this day, I don't know the reason why she wanted to break up. First, it was like, 'I think it's better to just be friends.' If I have to choose between losing her completely and being friends, then I'll be her friend. Fine. It's not what I want, but I'll settle for being friends.

"But for me, being friends means something. When I have a friend, we talk, I invite them out, and they invite me out. Apparently, for her, being friends means you can be nasty and mean and say cruel things if you want. So my 'friendship' lasted about a month.

"After that, we met three times in two weeks: hanging out, going to a party and going out to dinner. We went to a zoo too. During all of our three encounters, she was acting like we were still together. She was hanging on to my arm and holding me. She was confusing the hell out of me because she had told me she just wanted to be friends.

"She takes homestay students sometimes. She told me she had a new student coming at the end of the month. We made a plan to go on a trip to take pictures of the early cherry blossoms. I took a day off at my job. I had to ask in advance for this day off to go on the trip. First, we planned to go there for a couple of days. Then she changed her mind and said, 'Let's just do a day trip.'

"Later I was home and I came across the pictures from when we went to Okinawa. I picked a picture of me and her together, and sent it to her asking, 'Whatever happened to these people?' Her response to that was, 'You're such a girl!' I thought, *you know what? Fuck you!* I tried. I tried to be nice. I did everything. I said, 'If this is how you treat your friends, I don't want to be your friend. Just forget it. Don't talk to me anymore. Goodbye.'

"The next day, she unfriended me on Facebook and deleted me from Line. I tried to send her a message through Facebook, but it said, 'This person only allows friends.' So I tried Line, but it gave me a direct feedback saying, 'You can't send it to this person.' Then I sent a text through the phone. That went through. She was like, 'What do you want?' I said, 'Let's meet one last time and talk.' She said, 'OK, bye.'

"I went to meet her close to her house. Apparently, we couldn't be friends. We couldn't be lovers either. Since then, I haven't heard from her. I have no idea what she is doing now."

The artist

"A couple of weeks ago, I was helping out my friend because he was putting together his first live event. I went to meet him in Otsuka to go to the rehearsal. After that, we decided to have drinks at a bar.

"They had an event there that night. There were artists there and I met one of them. She handed me markers. I asked, 'What do you want me to do?' She said, 'Draw!' 'OK then, turn around.' I tried to draw on her. She was like, 'No, not on me!' Later, she took the marker and started drawing on my face. I was like, 'Fine, if you are going to draw on me, I'm going to draw on you.' Then we drew on each other. We exchanged Facebook contacts and then I went to my friend's concert.

"A couple of days later, I got a message on Facebook, 'Hey, what are you doing?' 'Nothing?' 'I'm in Shinjuku drinking. You want to come join me?' We met at the Hub (a British-themed bar). She introduced me to the people around. We were drinking and talking. I leaned that she was an artist and did amazing things. She'd never had an exhibition at all. At the pub, she was trying to get people to buy her work. So I said, 'Hey, I know a place where they give new artists a chance.'

"I was trying to figure out how to help her. Then, out of nowhere, she grabbed me, hugged me, and kissed me right on my neck. She was like, 'I'm happy. I feel good because you are doing this stuff for me. You seem like a nice guy.' OK, fine. We talked and drank some more. I looked at the time and I said, 'Fuck! I have to work tomorrow.' She said, 'I'll hang out here for a little longer.' She lived in Chiba, so she wasn't going to go home until the first train.

"But I was hungry. I said, 'You know what? I'm going to get a burger.' She decided to come with me. While I was leaving and taking a cab, she grabbed me and kissed me again. From what I've learned about Japanese women so far, if she's kissing me like that, there's one of two possibilities.

One: she wants to start a relationship. Two: she just wants to have sex. I thought, *OK, we'll meet again.*

"We decided to plan an event and started to meet a lot, hanging out and having dinner. Then we decided to go on an official date. I planned to go to Joypolis (an amusement park) in Odaiba.

"She was supposed to come over to my house on Thursday night. Friday was a holiday. She would stay, watch a movie, hang out, and the next morning we would go to Odaiba. But she changed her mind about coming to my house. She said, 'Let's just meet in Odaiba.' So we met in Odaiba.

"She just wasn't as friendly anymore. Before we went to Joypolis, I asked her, 'If you don't want to go here, we can do something else.' She wanted to go shopping in Odaiba. I said, 'OK, let's go shopping and have lunch or whatever.' But she said, 'Oh no, let's go to Joypolis.'

"We did some cosplay and that part seemed fun. We were supposed to meet another group of friends later in the evening, so we met them and had *monjayaki* in Tsukishima. We had a good time that night, but apparently she fell for my friend. I had no idea.

"I was going to New York in two days, but I didn't hear from her. I got to New York, but didn't hear from her at all. I looked at pictures that my friend posted on Facebook and there she was. Then I got another update of my friend hanging out with her in her hometown. I chatted with her online and she said, 'Well, he came to my studio. We had lunch with some of my old classmates and dinner with my parents.'

"OK, does that mean what I think it means? Usually, if you take someone home to meet your parents in Japan, that's a little bit serious. You don't just take anybody. She said, 'What do you think it means?' 'Are you dating him?' 'I don't know.' I was waiting for either yes or no. I asked, 'Did you kiss him?' She said, 'Yes.'

"We met and talked. According to her, she kissed everyone the same way. To her, it means greetings. What? You don't kiss everyone that same way! I've seen you meet people. I didn't see you kiss anybody else.

"I spoke to the guy and said, 'So what's going on?' He said, 'I don't know. We've been hanging out.' I said, 'You know, she did the same thing to me, so I was just wondering.' He said, 'I didn't know she was doing anything with you. I'm just going to back off.' I said, 'You don't have to. If I was even considering being serious, I couldn't continue now, because I can't trust her.' And he said, 'Yeah, I think I'm just going to back off.'

"I talked to her again. She told me she'd never had a boyfriend. She'd had sex-friends but never a boyfriend. She was twenty-five. I said, 'If you just want to have sex, that's fine, but tell people upfront.' She was like, 'OK. Sorry about that.'

"Then she told me she couldn't paint. We'd decided that we'd start a business. She was my flagship artist. Artists should do two things. One: paint as much as you can. Two: promote yourself. You talk to people about your work. You have to give them something. If you can't think of something, make it up! I said, 'I saw you talking to people that night at the Hub. That's what I want you to do.'

"She told me it was too difficult and that I asked too much. This was after telling me she thought she'd fallen in love with my friend. I said, 'OK, if you think you are in love with him, tell him. I'm not going to tell him for you this time. You're going to have to tell him.'"

The happiest relationship

"So here I am, going through the whole process again, except I'm a little less naïve now. I still inherently believe in people.

The problem is that, it's not all women. It just seems to be the ones I'm choosing. I told myself I'm not going to do anything with any woman that I meet at my usual bar, because it doesn't seem to work out.

"Two of the last not-so-good relationships were with people I met in that bar. And then there was one from somewhere completely different and not connected to that bar until I connected her. That didn't work out either. So I think I need to watch the pool that I pick from and never, ever bring a girl to the bar at all. At least until I see that everything is solid, set, and written in stone.

"Now when I meet people, I am suspicious. OK, what do you like? What is it you want? What's on your mind? Honestly, I have no idea. I tend to ask a lot of questions and my questions usually push them away, which for me is a good thing. If you can't stand up to my questions, then it won't last.

"If I can find women who understand and accept that, maybe I'll be happy. Until I do, I'll go out, have fun, and have a good time."

"Which was the happiest relationship in your life?"

"That would have been in Okinawa, I think. It was the second girlfriend. She was mellow and relaxing. There was no fuss, no complication, and no problems. We were just two people hanging out together. We saw each other on the weekend. And that was it."

Discussions

One thing we know about Andre is that he is quite capable of having a long-term relationship, given his six-year relationship with his late fiancée. However, it seems that he keeps meeting the wrong girls. One possible reason is that— as Andre points out—he dates girls from the wrong pool.

I also think that his being black and Jamaican-American attracts girls for the wrong reasons.

Andre said the jealous girl was constantly asking him if she was his girlfriend despite his six-month rule. Her reaction can be explained in the Japanese context. Japanese people tend to avoid uncertainty in relationships. In a lot of social interactions in Japan, everybody has a clear understanding of each person's social status. When Japanese people don't know what everyone's role is, they tend to feel very uncomfortable.

This also applies to romantic relationships. Normally, one person asks the other to be their girlfriend or boyfriend after several dates. The line is clear from the early stages of the relationship.

There's an expression in Japanese that says "more than friends, less than girlfriend or boyfriend," which is an ambiguous relationship and often has negative connotations. People tend to think that they should define the relationship clearly. The jealous girl might have felt unsettled because of this ambiguity.

With the single mother, Andre seems to have had constant miscommunication from the start. When she said, "We should hang out," she meant, "Ask me out," but Andre expected her to take the next step. When Andre said, "I can't eat pork, but you can," she didn't believe that he really didn't mind. When he took a photo with his friend, she saw some intentions that weren't necessarily there. When she wanted to break up with him, she sent a lot of non-verbal messages, but Andre needed her to express her intent verbally.

The thing is, Andre and the single mother have largely incompatible communication styles: Andre is literal and explicit, and the single mother is non-verbal and implicit. Andre must have felt that she read too much into things, and she must have felt that Andre was inconsiderate of her feelings. I don't think it's a question of who is right or wrong; they are simply different people.

He talked only briefly about the second girl in Okinawa. I wonder if it's because his relationship was so trouble-free that there wasn't much to talk about.

13. Leslie—when I woke up, he was holding my hand

How a Filipina girl inadvertently ended up with a Japanese guy

I MET LESLIE AT MY FRIEND's party. She had beautiful black hair and a slightly Middle Eastern look. I said 'Hi' to her and joined the conversation. But she was already talking to a guy.

His name was Masaki, and Leslie had met him earlier that night.

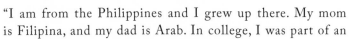

"I am from the Philippines and I grew up there. My mom is Filipina, and my dad is Arab. In college, I was part of an international organization for young people.

"A Japanese company was looking for global-minded young people because they wanted to expand their business abroad. They had a talk at my university and my friend forced me to attend. It was perfect for me. So after college, I ended up in Japan.

"The truth is, before coming to Japan, I didn't think I would date Japanese guys. I tend to fall for people who think like me—have strong opinions, are open-minded, and really global. I didn't have an image of Japanese guys being like that. I thought they loved their own culture too much and were effeminate. I really like traveling, and when I travel, I like staying in hostels. If I need to sleep on the floor in a foreign country, I will. I like eating street food. I want somebody who can do that with me. I thought Japanese guys would say, 'Oh my God, street food, no!'

"Last year, I attended a speed-dating event. Maybe I just wanted an ego boost, and wanted to see how many people would date me. I went out with one guy from the event. I thought he was cute. But he was a really typical *salary-man* (somebody who has a normal nine-to-five job) kind of guy, in the oil industry. He was stuck with his job, even though he hated it. He wanted to go out on expensive dates so he could impress typical girls. He was twenty-six, but he looked older. I didn't call him again.

"I hung out with another guy—a student from Tokyo University (the top university in Japan). It's kind of embarrassing, but I really liked him. He also grew up all over the world. He'd spent most of his life in South Africa. He was very smart and very witty. He had a very strange accent. I was really attracted to him.

"I met him at a meetup event—a night picnic in Yoyogi Park. We went to Harajuku and Shibuya with a bunch of other people. He was one of them. Actually, I had seen him at the event and thought he was interesting. But then the event was over, and I didn't have a chance to talk to him. But as we were walking, he started talking to me and we stayed out longer. We missed the train and walked around.

"We went out on dates and saw each other for two months. I could tell he was into me as well. But I don't know what his problem was. Maybe he was just one of those immature guys who didn't want to get into a committed relationship? I was disappointed because I really liked him. We just stopped talking to each other.

"The embarrassing thing is, I liked him enough to ask him out, even though I knew he would say no, which hurt my pride. He was kind of jerky about it. After that, I kind of gave up on dating in Japan. I thought that I would just make friends from now on. This story kind of hurts, but it's OK. I'm a big girl!"

Masaki

Then Leslie met Masaki at the party. It was apparent that they had hit it off well. People came into and left their conversation, but they always stayed together. They were paying attention to each other while other people were looking for somebody else to talk to.

"He was actually depressed at the time. Not super depressed, but he was on medication and seeing a therapist. He had just come back from Australia and had been in Japan for less than a year. He had been in Australia for three years. I just sensed goodness in him. He was really sincere. It's difficult to find sincerity nowadays. I had tried to date a couple of Japanese guys, but I didn't find the same sincerity in them.

"Masaki was really pure. Pure like cats and dogs, or babies you can't stop looking at. I guess that was what attracted me, but at that time, I didn't know that it was attraction. I just wanted to be friends with him. He liked hiking and I liked it too, so we would always go to parks and go hiking.

"I started wondering, *is this really just friendship? Are we dating?* I said to my friend, 'I don't know if I'm dating him or not.' Watching pandas eat bamboo in a zoo... that's a date, right?

"He would also bring some of his friends along. I've always craved the company of like-minded people. At my company, I have that. The people who got into the program with me were from all over the world. I'm good friends with them, but whenever we hang out, we just talk about the job. It's very tiring. So I was craving some other kind of interaction. Masaki always introduces me to his international friends.

"Then we went out to karaoke with my friends, for which I had invited him randomly. It became a regular thing: when I hung out with somebody, I always invited Masaki. That day, I got drunk because I had had too much wine, and then we went to karaoke. I was really tired and I started falling asleep on my friend's shoulder. But she just kept moving and I couldn't sleep. Masaki was beside me so I started falling asleep on him. When I woke up, he was already holding my hand. I thought, *OK, how did this happen?* I didn't really mind it though.

"After that, we went on a date in *Ni-chome*. He said, 'It is a surprise.' But I kind of knew where we were going. It was the first time I'd been to *Ni-chome*. He'd always told me about his gay friends. We went to a gay place and mingled with other people. Then, in the middle of *Ni-chome*, he told me he loved me!

"I was afraid at first because I'd never been in a serious relationship before. I would date guys, but I'd never thought of it as a serious thing. I was afraid of commitment at first. I thought it wouldn't be fun anymore. Masaki started saying, 'You are my girlfriend now.' I was thinking, *wait a minute.* I'm twenty-three. He's twenty-five. In our age group, you don't date seriously. It's always a casual thing. But Masaki is very romantic. He never dates anyone casually."

"Are you comfortable being in a serious relationship now?"

"Yeah. This is the first time in my life where I have imagined the future and had big plans."

"How would you describe him?"

"He's crazy. He's different. A lot of people describe him as different. My colleagues sometimes ask me if he is Japanese. I say, 'Yeah, he grew up here.' But they don't believe me.

"He used to be an IT guy, programming and making applications. But he got depressed and now he's doing something he's more passionate about, which is teaching. He just started a new job.

"The most difficult part of being with him is that when we Filipinos hang out, we like making jokes in our own language. We always have inside jokes. We are always hyperactive, but Masaki used to be an introvert, and he's very sensitive about being set apart from the group. At first, I tried integrating him into a group of my Filipino friends in Japan. But we would always argue afterwards. I would say, 'You just don't try hard enough,' or, 'You are too sensitive.'

"I love my friends and family, so it matters to me that Masaki integrates himself because I don't want to choose between him and my friends. It's kind of selfish, but I always divide my time for friends, work, and Masaki. When I set aside time for Masaki, I must meet him because I don't have any other time for him."

They went on a trip to the Philippines.

"We were taking a flight to the Philippines. We'd been dating for two months. We made it to the airport on time and got our boarding passes. I was hungry, so Masaki said, 'OK, let's go eat something.' We were having such a good time eating and drinking that we forgot the time. I thought the flight was at 1:30, so I thought we were still twenty minutes early. Apparently, our flight was at 1:15. We'd missed our flight.

"Most couples would fight in that situation, but we were really hippie people. We were cool about it. After that, we figured out that we had to go to Osaka first and take a flight to the Philippines from there instead of taking a direct flight from Narita. We took three days to do this and it took away most of my vacation. Well, it became a good story to tell. At least I know that when shit happens, we can still enjoy ourselves.

"In the Philippines, we went around to unconventional places. He asked me to take him to the slums. That really wasn't typical for a Japanese person. We went to the slums and he would talk to the people there. That made me really appreciate him more.

"Also in the Philippines, we climbed a mountain. I was drunk, and I was high. It was fun smoking stuff with him as well. We went to the beach and there was a mountain nearby. It was raining. We wanted to have an adventure. He really tried to keep me safe the entire time. It was really sweet.

"In Japan, he took me to his hometown and I met his family. It was cute to see how Japanese his family was, and also how much of an outcast Masaki was. I really understood his pain being such an outcast. We escaped his house and went hiking again. It got really dark, and it was just the two of us. We explored some areas where we were not supposed to go. I should have been scared, but I wasn't scared at all. I was really enjoying it."

"Were there any other memorable moments?"

"This also happened in the Philippines. It was our first day on the beach. I was with all my friends, and Masaki was with us. He started feeling isolated again, and got depressed along the way. He wouldn't talk to me properly for the rest of the day. It started getting kind of scary. He would shut off, which was really hard for me. Sometimes it would start out of nowhere. Right now, it's OK. He's not on medication anymore, and he's really functioning.

"When he is depressed, he doesn't talk about his feelings much. It's all inside. I just don't know what's going on or what to do. It doesn't happen often. Maybe three or four times during the entire time we've been together.

"But actually, he's quite healthy. I'm not really healthy. I used to drink too much. I used to eat out for every single meal. But right now, I don't drink or smoke much. I actually cook and eat vegetables. This is all because of Masaki. It's ironic because somebody with depression has had a more positive impact on my life than I have had on his.

"Things always change. Ever since I met Masaki, I've kind of gotten scared of change. I'm scared of not being able to stay here. I used to want to get transferred away from Japan, but now I'm not sure. I don't really know where this is going. I'm just trying my best to learn as much as I can right now. We always talk about the future. We both want to get out of Japan. Maybe New Zealand."

Discussions

I don't find Masaki particularly typically Japanese, except perhaps for his being a bit sensitive about what other people might say about him. In my opinion, he can be better understood as a guy who is into backpacking, yoga, and meditation rather than within the framework of a stereotypical Japanese guy. (He has been to Fiji and India, in addition to Australia and the Philippines. He also seems to attend yoga and meditation classes regularly.)

As for Leslie, her dream is to build a company that will represent the Philippines. She has had a hard time adapting to the Japanese work environment. When she expresses her opinions, the management doesn't take her seriously, because she's still young and new to the company. She's not fond of traditional Japanese values.

I get the impression that nationality and ethnicity don't play a big role in their relationship. Leslie doesn't seem to be particularly interested in Japan or in Japanese guys, and Masaki doesn't seem to be particularly interested in the Philippines or in Filipina women. Instead, they are both interested in dating people from different cultures in general, which totally works for them.

14. Lily—There's something I want to tell you

How a white American girl experienced Japanese-style dating

"I THOUGHT THERE WOULD BE NO dating life in Japan," Lily once told me. "I thought Japanese guys were not into white girls," she said.

Could she have been any more wrong?

Aiba-kun

"When I was in Nagoya as an exchange student, Japanese students came to our class once a week for about an hour to help us speak Japanese. I met Aiba-kun there, along with many other Japanese students.

"Aiba-kun always participated every week. I was studying Japanese literature and Aiba-kun's major was Japanese literature. So he talked to me a lot about Japanese literature and books he liked. I invited him to hang out with my friends a couple of times. I think at first he didn't really know what to think of me. He was kind of dorky and had never had a girlfriend before. He just liked books.

"Then, I could tell he was starting to like me. He wanted to be with me a lot. He invited me to his house. He was living with his parents and his sister. In Japan it's a really big deal when a guy invites a girl to his house, but I didn't understand that back then. I'm an American, and we always invite people to our houses. So I didn't think it was a big deal. But after I went to his house and met his family, things just kept on getting more intense.

"One day, we went to a pudding place where you could eat pasta and pudding. I knew something bad was about to happen. He said, 'There's something I want to tell you'. I thought, *oh, this totally is kokuhaku.* At that time, I didn't really know the *kokuhaku* culture that well. But I knew there was something going on. And of course he said, 'I'm in love with you and I want to be with you.'

"At the time, I had a boyfriend. It was a long-distance relationship because he was in the United States. So I said, 'Sorry, I have a boyfriend. I can't be with you.' But then I said, 'You know, you've never been on a date with a girl. I'm not going to be in Japan much longer. I'll go on a date with you and show you what a date feels like.' I think it was November then, and I was going back to the States in mid-December. So I had one more month left.

"Our 'date' was on a Saturday. We met at Nagoya Station. We went to a place called Inuyama which has one of the oldest castles in Japan. We went to the castle and walked around. While we were looking around outside the castle, he said, 'Can I take your picture?' Now I thought, *oh, this is so weird.* He took my picture, just me standing in front of the castle. Then we took the train back to Nagoya Station.

"We walked around Takashimaya (a department store). There was a macaroon store there. He asked, 'Do you want me to buy you a macaroon?' He was trying to show me he could spend money on me. I said, 'It's OK. I don't really like macaroons.'

"Then we went to the bookstore. Now things became more fun. He wasn't trying so hard to make everything date-like. Books were his comfort zone. We looked at a lot of books.

"By this time, it was evening. The place was very crowded because it was a Saturday. We went to this pasta restaurant. It was one of those restaurants in a department store that gets so crowded that everyone lines up outside. He had made a reservation. It was so funny, because it was not the kind of restaurant where you make a reservation. But he did. We had pasta and we talked a little bit. But it was awkward again because it was outside his comfort zone. Then I went home, and that was the end of the day.

"I continued to hang out with Aiba-kun because I thought he was a very interesting person, and I wanted him to be my friend. The last time we met before I went back to America, we went to see *Norwegian Wood*, a movie that had just come out. It was an awkward night because the movie was so disappointing for both of us. We just wanted to go home and cry.

"I was twenty-one and he was twenty. I don't think he understood the situation. You know, it was like anyone's first love. He was very obsessive. He'd say, 'I can't sleep because of you,' or, 'I feel sick because I love you so much.' I was thinking, *I don't have feelings for you, but I'll go on a date with you.* I don't think he ever will understand it. We are still friends, even though it goes on and off. Sometimes he says, 'I can't see you anymore,' but sometimes we can hang out.

"After I went back to America, we exchanged emails a little bit. But he only wrote in Japanese, and it was very hard for me because I didn't speak Japanese that well. It took me so long to write emails to him.

"I came back to Japan in September 2011 and moved here to Tokyo. The first person I met when I came to Japan was Aiba-kun. We met at Shinjuku Station, and we went on a four-day vacation together.

"He still really liked me then. But I wanted to be just friends with him. He was my only friend in Japan. It was really nice because he planned everything. He reserved a hotel, and planned which places we were going to go to. That was fun, but it was still really emotional for him.

"In my experience, people are more open with members of the opposite sex in America and Europe. I feel like he might have misunderstood some of those things. This American girl living in the States told me similar stories. Whenever she made friends with Japanese guys, they ended up thinking they were something more than friends. Some Japanese guys misinterpret it when American girls are just being friendly.

"In my case, it was probably because I gave him the time of day. I don't dismiss people just because they are dorky and geeky. He's not handsome, and he's abrasive sometimes. He doesn't have a great personality, and doesn't have good social skills. People think he's weird, but I was not the kind of person who would write him off just because he's weird. I was interested in his thoughts and the things he was interested in.

"When I went back to America, he sent me a really long letter in Japanese. I remember, in the letter he wrote, 'It was curiosity that first made me interested in you.' He was very interested in foreign things. We would see European movies together. He liked French literature a lot, and I also knew French literature well."

Lily studied in France before she came to Japan.

"There was this one thing that ultimately I was very disappointed about. I thought he was really, really smart, and had a lot of potential. I wanted to encourage him and so I said, 'You should think about going abroad.' But ultimately he didn't go abroad. I thought it could have really changed him as a person.

"He would say out of the blue, 'Do you know I'm angry with you?' When he gets angry about little things, he thinks it's my fault.

"I spent New Year's Eve with his family. It was really, really fun. Then in September, he came all the way to Tokyo and showed up at my house without telling me. It was my day off and I didn't have to work that day. He was saying, 'Please, be with me.' I said, 'I thought you understood that I wanted us to be friends. But if you can't deal with that, we're not going to talk anymore.'

"We didn't talk for seven or eight months. And then we started talking again. There's almost nobody in Japan who has known me since before I started working. He's one of the few people who does. The bond you have with people you meet before you start working is totally different from the bond you have with people you meet after that. If he could just get over his crazy, weird emotions, we'd be best friends. But I don't know if he will ever be able to grasp that it's OK to have a girl as a close friend, even if it's someone who he liked in the past.

"After we started talking again, he said he'd had sex with some girl. He said, 'It didn't mean anything.' He tried to use that to hurt me, but I just thought it was very stupid and childish. He tried to hurt me and wanted to make me aware of his pain."

Kokuhaku culture

"The *kokuhaku* thing has definitely been around quite a bit. There was a guy in my office last year who did the same thing. I think he was thirty. We worked together a little bit and I thought he was nice.

"Once, my roommates and I had a party with about fifteen of my friends at our house. He didn't have many friends in Tokyo, so I invited him. It was so awkward because he was being really weird. Everyone left to go home, but he didn't leave. It was a lunch party, and finished at four in the afternoon. But he didn't understand that the party was over. My friend and I had to go to the supermarket to get food, and he followed us around. We had to walk him to the train station to get rid of him.

"I had a feeling that he liked me. When we sent him on his way home, he gave me a hug. And it was a really awkward hug. He had lived in the United States for a long time, and it was as if he was saying, 'Oh, I understand that it's a part of American culture to give a hug.' My friend said, 'That was the most uncomfortable hug I've ever seen in my life! Stay away from him.'

"And then a couple of weeks later, it happened at work. He said the same line: 'There's something I want to tell you.' It's the exact same wording with every Japanese guy who is about to *kokuhaku*. I thought, *I need to run away right now!*

"It was outside the bathroom. He asked me, 'Do you have anything planned for this weekend?' I said, 'I'm kind of busy this weekend. So, goodbye!' I ran away.

"That Saturday, I was eating breakfast with my roommates as usual. I got a call on my work phone. It was him. He said, 'I'm near your house. Can you come out? There's something I want to tell you.' I understood what it was, but I said, 'If you want to talk about something, you can talk to me over the phone.' He said, 'No, please come out!'

"He was saying things like, 'I really want to be with you. I want to marry you. You're the most wonderful thing that's ever happened to me. I love you so much.' No, no, no. Weird, weird, weird. I had to talk to him for thirty minutes over the phone to get him to go away. It was really weird.

"There are all these Japanese girls who, I feel, are really strict. They have high standards. They want someone handsome who's earning a high salary. They are really picky. So, I feel like there are many guys who, if a girl is kind to them, become extremely happy and fall in love very easily. I think Japanese guys are not used to showing their emotions, so when a girl allows them to do that, it's like opening a floodgate of emotions. That's kind of dangerous."

"Have you ever come across an experienced Japanese guy?"

"In dating? No. But in Japan, even if you have a lot of experience, you don't talk about it with anyone else you date. I thought it was OK to talk about past experiences with someone you were dating. But in Japan, it's probably rude to laugh about horrible dates you had in the past. I can laugh about Aiba-kun all the time. It's not that I don't like him. It's just that my experience with him was a funny incident in my life. But if I talk about Aiba-kun to a guy who is traditionally Japanese, that will really hurt the guy."

The karaoke guy

"The next guy was one hundred percent Japanese. He was thirty-five. He liked Southern All Stars (a Japanese pop band) and sang really sappy seventies pop songs when we went to karaoke. He didn't speak English, and he wasn't really interested in foreign things. I was expected to be discreet and follow a lot of societal rules.

"I originally met him in the States. There was a Japanese community in Washington, D.C., where I went to university. He was working there.

"I met him through a Japanese friend. We went to karaoke with some friends and I flirted with him. I was asking, 'What songs do you want to sing?' And then when everyone kind of wanted to go home, I said, 'Let's go to your place.' So I went over to his house and slept over. It was more me who initiated the relationship. I don't think he would've initiated things like that."

"Was it that easy?"

"Ah, you just go for it. And they'll be surprised and be attracted to you. Then, a couple days later they'll do their own reciprocal mating ritual. Yeah, the best way is just to plough them over, and then they'll have no choice but to submit."

"Did he do the *kokuhaku* thing?"

"Yeah, of course he did. I think the fact that I made an approach with him made him do that. One day in the evening, he said he wanted to meet me to talk about something. And of course he said, 'There's something I want to tell you.' I thought, 'Yeah I've heard this exact expression many times before.' We went to a park and sat down. He said, 'I like you.' He gave me a letter and a really pretty pen. He said, 'I want you to be a very good writer. Please use this pen.' That was nice.

"It was romantic, but I didn't think it was really romantic at that time. Instead, I was more like laughing to myself, thinking, *oh, I'm going to be kokuhaku-ed again.* But that was a good *kokuhaku.*

"But *kokuhaku* is quite heavy. There's a difference between very traditional Japanese guys and guys who have been abroad. There was another guy who had a lot of overseas experience. When he and I hooked up, we were hanging out with a lot of friends, and we started talking because we had a lot of things in common. It was like, even though we were around other people, he was making sure we were always standing next to each other. We both understood that we were really attracted to each other. We didn't have to say anything. It was just like, *OK, everyone else leaves and we're going to go home together.* It was understood.

"But even with this guy, although I approached him and went home with him, he still had to do the *kokuhaku* after that. He needed to say, 'I like you and this is official.' I actually studied it in school. I think it's like a contract. It is a little bit like marriage. Japanese people don't want uncertainty in their life. I feel that in Japan, it's important what other people think of you. If you can't say definitely to the people around you that she's your girlfriend, that's weird too. Hence, 'There's something I want to tell you.'

"In America, relationships are often not clear and people get very frustrated. It's like, 'I want to be his girlfriend but he doesn't want to talk about it.' And that is also very stupid.

"So after I met him, we kept in touch. Then he came back to Japan and we hung out. We went out drinking, and got some good food. He was a Japanese history major, so we walked around historical areas in Tokyo. He explained a lot of Japanese history to me.

"In Japan, there is a lot of courtesy and manners that you have to show to the other person. Like, you wake up in the morning and send him a 'good morning' message. You go to bed and you text 'I'm going to bed.' It's very strict and rigid.

"It goes back to the idea that Japanese society in general isn't very comfortable with guys and girls being just friends. If I was to going to have a drink with a guy friend, I would have to lie to my boyfriend. Otherwise he'd say, 'Oh, be careful. They'll all start to like you.' That is something I don't really like."

"Did he show affection in public?"

"In front of people, no. That was out of question. In private, yeah. That was also kind of funny. There was so much resistance. But I think he had gotten less Japanese because of me. I think he was very uncommunicative about his emotions at first. If something was bothering him, he wouldn't say anything and instead, he would just get angry or sad about it. Or, he would be stressed at work and wouldn't say anything. So I pushed him to be more communicative. I had to tell him many times that it was OK to talk about his stress. Then he would talk about it, and it was better.

"But sometimes he forgot. It builds up and then there's a lot of stress. And that came out in the relationship. There were two incidents where he really got angry. I felt it was a cultural barrier or a misunderstanding. He was in D.C. and I was in Japan. There was a time difference, so we had to plan when we were going to talk.

"The first incident occurred when my friends from America had come to visit me in Japan. I took them out drinking one night. I had told him that I was taking them out. While I was out, he texted me saying, 'I have something that I really want to talk to you about. It's really important. We need to talk right now.' I saw it, but put my phone away.

"When I picked up my phone again, I saw that he had called me ten times. He called again and got really angry at me. My friends couldn't speak Japanese, so they didn't understand what we were saying, but we had a very big fight over the phone. He was saying, 'I had a really big thing that I wanted to talk to you about. Why don't you pick up your phone? You are terrible!'

"He'd had some meeting with his boss at work about his plans for the future. He'd told me about the meeting the day before, so I didn't think it was necessary to talk about it again. But he'd forgotten that he had told me all about it. He was so angry at me in front of everyone. He was screaming on the phone, and I tried to calm him down in Japanese. I told my friends that I had to go home. I was really upset. I didn't want to fight in front of everyone.

"And then the other incident occurred when I was having a very busy time at work. I was working very, very late, till three or four in the morning, and waking up at eight o'clock in the morning. One day, he called me up at midnight when I was finally asleep. He said, 'Something big happened.' I said, 'Are you OK?' He said, 'I got *kokuhaku*-ed!' That was the stupidest thing I'd ever heard! I was trying to sleep. I don't give two shits if someone *kokuhaku*-ed you. You obviously said no. Just call me tomorrow!

"He got so angry at me. He obviously thought that it was some critical life event that someone had *kokuhaku*-ed him. I'd worked with him to help him express his emotions, but sometimes they didn't come out in a constructive way. He was very manly. He liked to work out at the gym and he liked surfing. He studied World War II history. But once in a while, he would act extremely girly, and do things such as making a big deal out of being *kokuhaku*-ed.

"There was one other thing: if I were to marry him in the future, we would probably live in Japan, and then he wouldn't be able to speak English. The language we spoke when we were together was Japanese. But there were two parts of me: the Japanese part and the English part. So what would it be like to be with someone for your entire life who doesn't understand both parts of you? I spoke Japanese well enough, but it was nowhere near my level of English. There were definitely things I couldn't express in Japanese. And there are things I wouldn't express in Japanese, because it would be inappropriate, weird, or rude."

"Was he learning English at all?"

"Yeah, he was kind of OK. But you know, the problem is that if you start your relationship speaking one language, it's not going to change. So even if I say, 'Every Tuesday, we're going to speak in English,' it's not going to work. Besides, you want to speak the language you can communicate the fastest in with that person."

"So what happened after he got *kokuhaku*-ed?"

"He said, 'The worst part of being *kokuhaku*-ed was having to tell her I was divorced. She should never love someone who is divorced.' He thought getting divorced was shameful. We started dating while he was still married. He and his wife had a bad marriage, so it was a good thing they divorced. But the fact that he thinks being divorced makes him damaged goods is very strange and really silly. That made me think that he didn't have the same values as I do.

"After that, we didn't talk very much. And then we went on a trip together in the beginning of March. We went to California together. I planned everything for this fucking trip! I booked the hotel, booked the car, found restaurants. He couldn't do any of these things himself, because he couldn't speak English. I don't really speak Japanese that well, but I still reserve restaurants and book hotels, right? It's not that hard. But that's OK. I wanted to have a really good vacation. It was going to be perfect.

"We were going to meet in San Francisco and drive to Los Angeles. I arrived at the airport Friday afternoon. The first thing I did was call him. I couldn't use my Japanese cell phone in America, so I used the airport Wi-Fi. I said, 'I'm here. I'm safe. I'm going to go to the hotel now and have dinner with my friend. I'll see you tomorrow.' Then I had dinner with my friend, went back to the hotel, and fell asleep.

"The next day, I woke up. His flight was supposed to come in very early in the morning. I thought he would be at the airport, so I gave him a call. I said, 'Are you here? I'm so excited! I'm waiting for you.' He called me back in five minutes and said, 'Hey, I'm here. I arrived, but I'm going to go home. I'm leaving.'

"I asked, 'What's wrong? Are you OK?'" He said, 'No. You didn't text me after you went back to the hotel last night. And you didn't text me this morning either. You're a terrible person. I'm going back.' I said, 'No. I planned this whole vacation! I'm here in America. What am I going to do?' And he hung up on me! I was crying and fighting in Japanese over the phone in the hotel lobby in front of everyone.

"Eventually he came, but he was just so angry. I wanted him to meet my friend because it was important to me that my boyfriend met my friends. I understood that he wanted time for us to be alone, but I also wanted him to meet my friends. But he was really angry over meeting them. He was embarrassed and stressed about the fact he couldn't speak English very well.

"Then we went on a road trip together and started driving to Los Angeles. We got coffee somewhere and he said, 'You never asked me about my divorce. Why didn't you? Everyone asks about my divorce.' Well, his divorce wasn't my business and I hadn't needed to ask him about it. Then he said, 'You are just jealous about my ex-wife.' It was really terrible. Screaming and fighting again.

"I came back to Japan. I didn't want to talk to him very much. I needed space, and he understood that. But after thinking about it, I realized that he was under a lot of stress at work and didn't know how to deal with it. That was why he had said to me that I was a terrible person. That's so silly. He should be able to deal with stress at work, and he should be able to talk about his problems.

"Finally, I said to him, 'Look, I think we need to break up.' If your boyfriend tells you every day that you are a terrible person and that he hates you, that sucks, right? So I said, 'We can't be together anymore.' And he said, 'You know, that means we can never talk again and you're just going to be like a complete stranger to me!'

"We didn't talk for three months after that. But here's the weird thing. As we were talking during the break-up call, he asked, 'So, what am I going to do with your stuff?' That was the last thing on my mind. I said, 'I don't know. Just throw it away.' A week later, a huge box arrived at my house—no return address. Every single present I'd ever gotten for him was there. Creepy. Don't send them to me! It must have cost hundreds of dollars to send them to Japan from America. The box was so big, a human being could have fit inside."

The Blackberry guy

"After that, I went to Hong Kong for a company orientation. There was a guy in the Hong Kong office who had worked in Japan before. He was thirty-three and spoke fluent English. He had gone to graduate school in America. I had never formally met him before, because when I joined the company in Tokyo, he was just leaving for Hong Kong. I was given the Blackberry he'd used in Tokyo, and it became mine. He was very well known in the company, and everyone liked him. But I always got calls on my Blackberry at six o'clock in the morning from people who were looking for him.

"So when I went to Hong Kong, I was finally going to ask him for his phone number and his contact information so that if those people called again, I could give it to them. We had lunch, but it was kind of boring. Then that night, everyone had drinks and he was there too. He started talking about Haruki Murakami. It turned out he liked Japanese literature. We had all this stuff in common. It was really amazing to find someone who spoke both Japanese and

English and liked Japanese literature. So, we had some sexy times after. But then he said, 'I'm sorry, I have a girlfriend.' She lived in England. So that was just one night.

"The next day, he said, 'Let's hang out again.' Then the day after, we had dinner together. I asked, 'Can I sleep over at your house?' He said, 'No, I have a girlfriend. Sorry.' But after I returned to Japan, we kept talking on Facebook. It was really fun. We talked every day. We Skyped a couple of times and finally I asked him, 'So do you still have a girlfriend? Because if you do, this is really inappropriate.' He said, 'No, actually we broke up.' I thought, *why didn't you tell me sooner?*, but I said, 'OK. I really like talking to you, so let's keep talking.'

"He is so fastidious and all he cares about is his clothes, his apartment, his hair, and his glasses. On weekends, he wears the same jeans and the same T-shirt. He buys about fifty pairs of them—the same ones because he thinks they are fashionable.

"I'm always the one who takes initiatives. If I don't say 'I'm going to Hong Kong,' he won't ask me to come to Hong Kong. Usually I don't have to chase guys. Guys chase me. But if I like someone, then I'll definitely take initiative because you have to find out if your feelings are real. You can't know how you really feel unless you spend time with someone.

"So in June, I really wanted to see him, and I really wanted to know whether I should pursue him or not. We had been talking about going to see each other, but he wasn't making any plans. So I said, 'OK, this weekend, I'm coming to Hong Kong whether you like it or not.' So I went there and we had a fun weekend. It was really good. We were together the whole time. He took a day off from work so we could spend more time together.

"Then I asked him, 'So, do you want a girlfriend?' But I meant in general. Not me. He said, 'I don't know. I kind of want to find a girlfriend in Hong Kong. I'm looking around, but knowing me, I probably won't find one, because I'm lazy.' He used to send me really fun stuff like movies on Facebook, but after that, he communicated less and less. When I got back to Japan, I sent him a couple of nice emails saying, 'I'm thinking of you. That was really fun, and thank you.' He didn't reply. We still talked a little bit, but he just got more and more distant.

"Then I went to visit him again in July and we spent the weekend together. He introduced me to one of his really cool friends. But he didn't tell his friend that he and I liked each other, or that we were kind of in a relationship. Over dinner, his friend asked me, 'So, do you have a boyfriend?' I thought, *I guess not!* But he was right there! He could've said something, right? It was so embarrassing.

"I was there for three days and on Monday, he had to go to work. So I spent the whole day doing some of my work and making him Japanese curry. I made curry noodles and extra curry so that he would have enough for the week. He was really excited and said it was really good, but didn't say thank you. And then a month later, we were talking again. I told him, 'Oh yeah, so the other day, I went on a date,' which was true. And then all of a sudden he said, 'Oh my god! By the way, your curry was really good.'

"The last night I was there, I had to take a late flight at midnight. He came home from work about eight pm and had some curry. Then I asked, 'So, do you want to have sex before I leave?' He was saying, 'I don't know, there's not a lot of time.'"

"Do you think it's true that Japanese guys are passive in bed?"

"With him, that's exactly the case. But the one before him had a lot of sex drive. It was almost a problem. He wanted to have sex a lot more than I did, like, three times a day. But he was good. We also really liked each other.

"With another ex-boyfriend, it was a really positive experience. We both thought it was good to talk about what we could do to make things better. That was really, really good. But it was also because I pushed him to talk about these things a little bit. Once he got to communicating, it was better."

Discussions

Kokuhaku is one of the most important concepts in Japanese dating culture. Again, many Japanese people prefer to define relationships clearly, and *kokuhaku* serves this need. Sometimes, Japanese people even start a relationship by explicitly stating that it is with the intent of getting married.

I think Lily's experience is quite close to most Japanese girls' experiences in Japan. She speaks fluent Japanese and meets guys the way many Japanese women would: through school, through friends, and at workplaces—the top three places where Japanese people meet their spouses.

The karaoke guy's emotional dependence seems extreme, but I think there's a cultural explanation for it. Japanese guys are often used to having their mothers take care of them (as Sean, the British buy, remarked) and some guys look for motherly qualities in their girlfriends. The karaoke guy seemed to get angry when he didn't get the attention he thought he deserved. This can be interpreted as a childish sense of entitlement.

Can Japanese guys just be friends with girls? I would say that they can. As a Japanese guy, I have (or have had) Japanese female friends in whom I'm not romantically interested. Also, I've known plenty of Japanese guys who had Japanese female friends. (Actually, the other day, a girl from Osaka told me that she tended to fall in love with her guy friends who wouldn't reciprocate her feelings.) My guess is that Lily tends to meet guys who don't have much experience with women in general, or who simply become jealous because these women are very nice and friendly people.

Epilogue

When culture matters

"**O**VERALL, I DON'T THINK INTERCULTURAL or interracial relationships are any different from other relationships. You have to work at them anyway," Kala said.

I think that this is a beautiful thought on which to end this book. Many times, in the end, who you really are is all that matters, regardless of culture.

However, I also think that there are cultural differences between Japan and many western countries, and understanding them will make your dating life a bit easier.

Kokuhaku, or the confession of love

Take Julia's experience: she is an American woman married to a Japanese guy. She recalls the time when he dropped the L bomb. She had already been hanging out with him for a while at university.

"I came back to campus and told him that I left my boyfriend. He was *very* surprised. He invited me to see a movie and try some wine at his apartment. I said yes. After the movie, we started playing with his cats. Then he started tickling me. Then he kissed my neck. I kissed his cheek. And next thing I knew I was on my back and we were kissing a lot. It was rather fast!

"Then he did that confession thing, which is supposedly a very Japanese thing to do, or so I've been told. He asked me to be his girlfriend; I said yes. He told me he loved me and I almost ran out the door. In America, we don't say 'I love you' very quickly. We wait until we're a thousand percent sure, and it takes a while. Most American women would have run out the door in this situation."

This "confession thing" is *kokuhaku*. To *kokuhaku* is to say that you like somebody romantically and want to be in a relationship with them. Typically, *kokuhaku* happens towards the end of the third date. You say something like, "I like (or love) you. Would you be my girlfriend (or boyfriend)?" If the other person says yes, you are officially a couple.

Kokuhaku seems to be the standard procedure for Japanese people. When they start going on dates, their big concern is how to do a *kokuhaku*. Japanese women often talk about whether they should *kokuhaku* themselves or wait for guys to do it. A lot of dating advice in Japan is centered on *kokuhaku*.

Kokuhaku is not always obvious if you are new to Japan. When Natasha, the Russian girl, dated her first Japanese boyfriend, he did a *kokuhaku*, but he had to explain it. She thought that he was just saying casually that he liked her.

Lily, the American girl, experienced *kokuhaku* so many times that she can tell when a guy is about to do it. According to her, guys always say, "There's something I want to tell you," before proceeding to *kokuhaku*.

On the other hand, not *all* Japanese people do *kokuhaku*. For example, I don't do it, because I've never liked the concept. I think it's a bit too ritualistic for my taste.

How Japanese people talk

I studied in France for one year and would often hang out with French people from the same university.

I remember being at a small party at my friend's house, getting frustrated because I couldn't participate in the conversation. Everybody seemed to be talking non-stop.

If you observe Japanese people talking, you may realize that when they finish talking, they often pause briefly to see if other people want to join in. Sometimes they say, "So, what do you think?" to encourage the other person to talk. It is often considered the speaker's responsibility to give other people the chance to talk.

This didn't always happen in France. I would expect a pause, but it never came. I couldn't tell whether they had finished talking or not.

My communication improved when I remembered a book I had read a long time ago called *That's Not What I Meant*, by Deborah Tannen. Tannen argues that different cultures use different pacing and pauses. In some cultures, people don't pause when they finish talking. If a listener wants to speak, they expect him to jump in and take over the conversation. Otherwise, the speaker will search for another topic and continue. It's considered the listener's responsibility to speak up if they have something to contribute.

It was hard for me to speak up when other people were still talking, because doing so felt as though I was interrupting. But after a while, I realized that others took my "interruption" quite positively and the conversation would become livelier and more interactive.

Frank, the American guy, is a very good example of the non-pausing conversational style.

"I need to listen more," Frank said. "My ex-wife said, 'It's hard because you don't listen.' My mom finishes people's sentences all the time. There's never any silence in my family. Whoever speaks the loudest gets to talk. I'm very uncomfortable with silence. I'm getting better, but that makes me less American. If I go home, people will ask, 'Are you OK?' because I'm too silent."

Michelle, the Finnish girl, had the opposite style: she takes long pauses. When I interviewed her, I tried not to interrupt her, because her pauses were longer than what I was used to.

If you are from a faster-paced culture, try slowing down and pausing when you talk to Japanese people. These simple changes should improve your communication a lot.

What Japanese people never say

Recently, I worked on a project that involved multiple Japanese companies at my day job. At meetings, they would always talk about the client's feelings rather than the project itself. They would say, "The client seemed upset during the last meeting. That guy's voice was slightly shaky. Maybe we should withhold some information until he calms down."

Japanese people tend to pay a great deal of attention to other people's non-verbal messages. They are trained to do so. When somebody fails to decode a non-verbal message, they tend to blame the listener for not being able to read the speaker's hidden intentions.

Kala, the American girl married to a Japanese husband, talked about the "automatic translator" that decodes her husband's non-verbal cues. When he is not happy with something, he has indirect ways of showing his feelings.

"He won't say he's hungry. If he's hungry, he comes to the kitchen and starts asking me questions. If I'm cooking, he will say, 'Do you need some help?' I use my 'automatic translator' to understand that he actually means 'I'm hungry.'"

Julia, also an American woman, learned during the course of her marriage how to deal with her non-expressive Japanese husband.

"Right now, we are struggling financially, so it's been stressful," she says. "He takes that stress out on me sometimes, without realizing it. I've figured out that if he gets upset and takes it out on me, and then if I leave him alone, he feels bad and then apologizes and comes back to me. This shows him what he did wrong. I think that's the main lesson for me, lately. Showing. Not telling. Talking doesn't always work. He said it would work so I tried it. But it didn't work.

"It really wasn't until late into year two of living with my husband, that I started getting gut feelings about how he was feeling, based on little things he would do. Like the difference between a 'normal' level of quiet versus an 'abnormal' level of quiet, energy level, or facial expressions. And since he didn't express his emotions in the beginning, I've become pretty good at it. It's like being a blind person who can hear really well."

A couple of days ago, I took a flight with ANA. I wasn't used to Japanese airlines, because I usually choose cheaper ones. I noticed that they would bring me tissues because I was sneezing, even though I didn't ask for anything. The flight attendants just assumed I needed tissues (which I did) and brought them to me without asking me if I needed them.

I happened to take one more ANA flight from Germany. It was a connecting flight. When I arrived in Germany on another flight, I noticed an Asian guy holding a sign indicating the name of the flight. I wasn't sure what he was doing, but it turned out that he was there to walk Japanese customers to the next gate. To me, it felt as though ANA was "over-parenting" Japanese customers.

These are interesting examples of Japanese "mind-reading." Japanese people are often expected to read other people's minds and act upon them. This can be a problem in a multicultural relationship because in some other cultures, people are expected to speak up instead of waiting for somebody to notice something. It is important to understand your partner's communication style.

"I wouldn't marry a foreigner"

I went to a photo shoot the other day. When the stylist was fixing my hair, I talked about this book. She was interested. I asked her about her experience with non-Japanese guys. Apparently, she had dated American, British, and Japanese-Brazilian guys.

"So, do you prefer Japanese guys or Western guys?" I asked.

"Well, foreign guys are fun to date, but if I was going to get married, I would choose a Japanese guy," she said.

Refusing to marry a non-Japanese guy? That doesn't sound great. It reminds me of what Nadia told me: "I didn't like being strung along, because too many people in Japan are in a relationship for a long time, and then after five or six years the other person drops the bomb and says, 'I can't marry a non-Japanese person.'"

Nadia did end up marrying the guy because he was open to marriage from the start, but if you are thinking of marrying somebody who is Japanese, you might want to make sure that the other person is truly up for international marriage.

James, the British guy who saved the Japanese girl from a robber, said, "Some girls' parents didn't let them date a foreigner, so they slept with foreigners until they were twenty-seven and then, suddenly, they broke up with them and the next day they would marry a Japanese guy."

Japanese people in bed

I went on a date with a Japanese girl who was very horny. We went to Odaiba, a sort of cheesy dating spot in Tokyo. At the mall, she was already touching my butt. I went to the bathroom and she said half-jokingly, 'Let's go in there together!' But in retrospect, I don't think she was really joking.

That night, we went to a love hotel (obviously), but there was one thing that wasn't quite right. As horny as she was, once she was in bed, she seemed to lose her momentum and just lie there like a doll. She did say things like 'I'm so wet,' but her body remained immobile.

There is a word for this in Japanese: *maguro*—literally, "tuna." To be *maguro* is to be very passive in bed. This, of course, is considered a bad thing, even in Japan. Guys sometimes complain that their girlfriends are *maguro*.

A lot of people in this book have had similar experiences. Joshua, the Kenyan guy, said, "[Japanese girls] are not good in bed. They lie down and wait for you to do something. There was only one girl in Okayama who was really good in bed. She was active. The other girls I had in Japan didn't have any moves."

Natasha, the Russian girl, said, "Well, I've dated two Japanese guys and of course we had sex. I'm really sorry to say this, but both of them were not good in bed." Natasha explained that "size doesn't really matter, but technique does. I say I'm a very active person in bed, but when I started moving and tried to do something, they kind of freaked out. They were like, 'What are you doing? Get back!'"

Fortunately, you also come across people who have a good sex life in Japan. Sabina, the Russian model, said, "You know, for me, [my sex life] is the best thing. I cannot talk about Japanese guys in general, because I haven't had a lot in my life, but my husband is best for my body and for my feelings. It's maybe why our marriage stays alive. He knows my body."

Lily, the American girl said, "With another one of my ex-boyfriends, it was a really positive experience. We both thought it was good to talk about what we could do to make things better. That was really, really good."

Talking about sex

While sexually tolerant, Japanese people often don't like talking about sex in public. Natasha, the Russian girl, faced a clerk who was extremely reluctant to talk about condoms in a sex shop.

I had the opposite experience in Germany. I went into a random sex shop and I asked one of the staff why German porn was so famous. She was completely cool with my question and explained to me that German people were comfortable with sex because they always talked about it openly. Therefore, they were relatively less hesitant when it came to being in porn.

I have another story about the sex shop in Akihabara, an area in Tokyo famous for its nerd culture. Sandra Daugherty, an American sex educator, went there and learned that she would get a 20% discount if she let them take a photo of her wearing sexy lingerie. She was interested, but she wasn't sure if she should.

She left the shop, but couldn't forget about the photo. As a sex educator, she felt almost compelled to do it. So she went back to the shop, bought some lingerie, and asked them to take her photo.

They were incredibly hesitant.

Seeing that she didn't speak Japanese, they explained the concept to her over and over again, showing photos and pointing to stuff. They almost seemed to be ashamed of the whole thing.

When they finally agreed, they closed off the entire floor. They locked the door and pulled the blinds down on the windows so no one could see. They took extreme care just for a couple of Polaroid photos of a half-naked girl.

Different sides of a story

Every story has more than one side.

Consider this short story.

A robber killed a man. The robber wanted the man's wife.

According to the robber, he befriended the man and lured him to a mountain. He tied the man up and raped his wife. The man's wife said, "Either you kill my husband or he kills you." So the robber untied the man and they had a sword fight. The robber won, but the wife had run away. Or so he says.

But the wife has a different story. After the robber raped her, she fainted. When she woke up, the robber was gone. She wanted to die along with her husband because of the shame. She intended to kill her husband first and then kill herself, but after killing her husband, she got cold feet. She ran away. Or so she says.

But then the dead man tells a whole different story...

What you read above is actually a short story called "In a Grove" by Ryunosuke Akutagawa. The famous film *Rashomon* is based on this story. It became a classic because it does an excellent job capturing how people see the same things differently.

Take the story of Andre, the ex-Marine. His ex-girlfriend had completely changed when she got back from her trip to Egypt. She became very distant and started avoiding him.

To me, it is apparent that she lost romantic interest in him at some point during or prior to the trip. The problem was, she didn't know how to communicate that to him. While she was in love with him, small things didn't bother her too much. Sure, he didn't eat pork (her favorite meat), and he wasn't able to guess her true intentions when she said she was OK with not taking the ropeway on their trip, but she didn't mind, because she liked him. However, once she stopped liking him, those same things started to annoy her. That's just how feelings work.

But my editor has a different angle. She says, "By being so inflexible with his personal rules, he hadn't really learned to adjust his relationship style to fit Japanese dating culture or his individual girlfriends' personal rules. With the girlfriend who went to Egypt, it sounds like he didn't really figure out that she was being less direct with him regarding what she wanted. When she said 'I want to go up the hill, but I'll go home if you want to,' she really meant 'I want to wait and go up the hill,' but he only heard 'I'll go home if you want to.' And when he said he couldn't eat pork, but she could if she wanted to, she interpreted that as 'No pork, please,' even though he really meant that she could eat it!"

There are already two interpretations of the same story.

You may find it interesting to discuss the stories in this book with people around you. If you are in a relationship, this can be a perfect opportunity to learn about each other's way of seeing things.

The best thing about stories is that you can learn from them. I hope this book will help you improve your dating life in Japan.

A Message from the Author

Dear readers,

Hi, I'm Yuta. Thank you very much for reading this book. It's been nearly a year since I came up with the original idea while traveling on Narita Express on my way to Jamaica, and I am extremely proud of being able to publish it.

As mentioned earlier, you can download an extra chapter for free! The chapter is titled *Takuya and Annie—If you really like her, you won't give up easily* and you can download it for free at:

http://www.yutaaoki.com/ts-extra

If you enjoyed this book, please subscribe to my newsletter at http://www.yutaaoki.com/sub-ts so you don't miss out on anything!

If you want to send me a direct message, you can reach me at http://www.yutaaoki.com/blog/contact

You can also find me on various social media:
Blog: http://www.yutaaoki.com/blog/
Twitter: https://twitter.com/ThatYuta
YouTube: https://www.youtube.com/user/YPlusShow/
Facebook: https://www.facebook.com/YutaAokiOfficial
Quora: http://www.quora.com/Yuta-Aoki

Hope to see you soon!

Yuta Aoki
Winter 2014

Acknowledgments

I would like to thank every single person I interviewed for this book. Unfortunately, I couldn't include all of you in this book, but I'm very thankful to each and every one of you. Without you, this book would never have been possible.

I would like to thank Kimberly Ito, Rebecca McLeod, Yolande McLean, and Gisela Dixon for awesome editing. You guys have exceeded my expectations. I am so grateful that you spotted so many mistakes and made helpful suggestions.

Special thanks to Indika Udayanga, Maricris Rezai Yoshida, Kazuaki Yoshida, Yuri Akamine, Yohan Tanaka, Kendal Kiehne, Jenya, Daniel Robson, Ala' Saturnino Omar, Alison Rodgers, John Francis, Karen Amendolagine, Yana, Najwa Waheed Naohara, Ayaka Kato, Cecilia Grandi, and Eleanor Warnock for inspiration, helpful feedback, and encouragement.

About the Author

Yuta Aoki is a chronic traveler. He has been to more than thirty countries, from Eastern Europe all the way across to Southeast Asia. He enjoys talking to local people and listening to their stories. His desire to share the best of these stories inspired him to write *There's Something I Want to Tell You: True Stories of Mixed Dating in Japan.*

He dates internationally, although he's slightly worried that he might end up spending more time writing about dating than actually doing it.

He was born and raised in Japan. For more information, visit his website at www.YutaAoki.com. He would love to hear from you.

90293691R00138

Made in the USA
Columbia, SC
01 March 2018